CHRISTMAS!

The Biblical, Empirical, And Revelational

EVIDENCE

Is Jesus Really The Reason For The Season?

PASTOR CLIFF MCANTHONY

CONTENTS

ACKNOWLEDGEMENT

I acknowledge and thank the Almighty God, our LORD and Savior Jesus Christ, for the inspiration, wisdom, and grace to accomplish the writing of this book. I am really blessed and amazed by God's support and presence through it all. I give all glory to God Almighty, who has been involved in the writing of this book from the very start. God graciously gave me the conclusion for this book through a prophetic revelation on my birthday on August 30, 2025. I guess the LORD gave me a birthday gift. I am truly grateful to Him for His active involvement in my writing of this book and others. Through God's grace, the completion of this book has made it my sixth book in about two years. May the name of our LORD, my Savior Jesus Christ, be praised forever, Amen.

I also want to acknowledge and appreciate my mother, Mrs. Josephine Ihejirika, who made herself available for God to use, for the prophetic revelations recorded in this book. And also, for God to use her to support me in various ways, especially spiritual support. You have been a tremendous source of spiritual support and inspiration to me through your prayers, godly fear, and spiritual dedication to God. I love you, and I am very grateful to God for a mother like you. May the Almighty God continue to bless and grant you all your heart's desires in this life and heaven at last, in Jesus' name, Amen. Finally, I would like to acknowledge

1

Christmas!

my brothers and sisters in Christ who have been very supportive and encouraging. My book-writing journey and successes cannot be written without mentioning you. Your contributions, suggestions, encouragement, patronage, and reviews were all instrumental to my success as an author. May the LORD continue to support, encourage, bless, and grant you all heaven at last, in Jesus' name, Amen.

PREFACE

This book addresses the tradition of observing and celebrating Christmas. It focuses on the biblical, empirical, and revelational evidence for the December 25th Christmas celebrations. The Bible: "Basic Instruction Before Leaving Earth" is both a spiritual and a historical book. Being a book of historical records, the Bible has accurate accounts of key events with varying levels of detail. Hence, what records does the Bible have on the birth date and birthday celebration of our LORD and Savior, Jesus Christ? Part one of this book covers the biblical record for the birth date and birthday celebration of our LORD and Savior, Jesus Christ. It reviews the details of Jesus's birth in two parts: (1) the eyewitness accounts and (2) the prophetic revelation accounts. It examines the biblical evidence for Christmas, that is, the scriptural historical evidence for Jesus' birth date and birthday celebration. Since the Bible is our USA (Ultimate Source of Authority) for reference to truth. The book examines scriptural evidence to understand the truth and basis for December 25th, as a day to remember and celebrate the birth of Jesus. Although the world is filled with evidence of how pagan practices metamorphosed into Christmas through the Catholic Church. And eventually made their way to the mainstream Protestant churches. Nonetheless, this book did not reference any extrabiblical sources for the pagan origin of the Christmas celebration. Not because those claims and sources are not credible. Rather, it is to focus solely on the Bible, the Ultimate Source of Authority for truth for all heavenly-minded Christians.

"The Biblical Evidence" examined the biblical records of Jesus' birth for the evidence of His birth date and birthday celebrations. Since the Bible is the Ultimate Source of Authority for reference to truth in Christianity. The book reviewed the historical and scriptural truth about the birth of Jesus to understand the basis for and the relevance of the December 25th Christmas celebration in Christianity. The careful examination of biblical records revealed no evidence for the date of Jesus Christ's birth. And also revealed no evidence for the December 25th Christmas celebration or for any other day. The only logical conclusion that could be drawn from the biblical records is that God deliberately withheld revealing the birth date of Jesus. And because it was unprofitable for the Christian faith, holiness, and eternal life.

Part two deals with the empirical evidence, that is, facts and knowledge gained through experience and observation without using scientific methods or theory. Empirical evidence can be put together by a layman on any subject matter. The Empirical Evidence is all about what we have observed and experienced. It is not about what was written or reported in times past, or what someone has taught, or some scientific theory. Rather, it's about my observations and experiences, yours, and those of others. And without a shadow of doubt, these observations and experiences speak louder than words. "The Empirical Evidence" examined our contemporary history of the December 25th Christmas celebrations. That is, the observable evidence in our lifetime to understand why Jesus never revealed His birthday.

Preface

Neither celebrated it nor commanded His followers to celebrate it. Examining the things we have observed and experienced about the ways the Christmas season is portrayed, promoted, and celebrated. Can we say that Jesus Christ is really the reason for the season? Based on your observations and experiences since the time you learned of the celebration of Christmas to date. The things you have seen, heard, and experienced, could you conclude that Jesus is really the reason for the season? The first empirical evidence considered is the secular world. The secular world holds a lot of irrefutable empirical evidence for why Jesus never revealed His birthday nor commanded Christians to commemorate and celebrate it.

Part 3, "The Revelational Evidence," affirms the biblical truth about the December 25th Christmas celebrations through revelations. Genuine revelations are God's Word to His people in the present. They could either come through prophecies, dreams, visions, or an audible voice. Genuine revelations will not contradict God's Word; they always validate and give clarity to God's written words in the Bible. Any revelation that contradicts the Bible is not from God. The Bible is our USA, i.e., "Ultimate Source of Authority," for reference to truth. The truth about Christianity and life in general is found in the Bible. The Bible is a compilation of God's revelations to forty different authors of various backgrounds and geographic locations over a period of about 1,500 years. The Bible, "Basic Instruction Before Leaving Earth," is God's Word to humanity. It is the book that reveals all the truth about life and its purpose. All truth claims in life that contradict the Bible are false claims, be they religious or scientific. The Bible validates the authenticity and relevance of revelations and prophecies in contemporary times.

John 16:13-14

13Howbeit when he, the Spirit of truth, is come, he will guide you into all truth: for he shall not speak of himself; but whatsoever he shall hear, that shall he speak: and he will shew you things to come. 14He shall glorify me: for he shall receive of mine, and shall shew it unto you.

1 Thessalonians 5:19-21

19Quench not the Spirit. 20Despise not prophesyings. 21Prove all things; hold fast that which is good.

Jesus says in John 16 that He will send us, His followers, the Spirit of truth to guide us into all truth. He said that the Spirit will not speak anything contrary to the course of Jesus Christ, and will only glorify Him. Then, in Thessalonians 5, Christians were admonished not to quench the Spirit of truth and should not despise prophecies. They should prove all prophecies and hold on to good prophecies, i.e., those in line with the Bible. The importance of prophecies and revelations in the Christian journey is astronomical. However, some Christians claim that prophecies/revelations ended with the Apostles and have ceased after the Apostolic era. This is a false claim because it contradicts the Bible and the very essence of Jesus Christ, and does not glorify Him. Hebrews 13:8, *"Jesus Christ the same yesterday, and to day, and for ever."* The Bible says that Jesus is the same yesterday, today, and forever. Therefore, if He gave revelations yesteryears during the Apostolic era, He will also give revelations today because He is the same forever. Jesus said that when the Holy Spirit comes, He will speak, John 16:13. *"Howbeit when he, the Spirit of truth, is come, he will guide you into all truth: for he shall not speak of himself; but whatsoever he shall hear, that shall he speak: and he will shew you things to come."* Then, how come these Christians are claiming that the Holy Spirit can no longer speak? The question should be, what has the Holy Spirit revealed in our time about the December 25th Christmas celebrations? The Revelational Evidence unveils chilling divine revelations on the December 25th Christmas celebrations. God's revelation and conclusion on the Christmas celebrations in this book is a reawakening call to Christians. These revelations will cause any heavenly-minded Christian to fear God and realign their positions on Christmas celebration.

Part 1

The Biblical

Evidence

CHAPTER 1

BIBLICAL RECORDS OF
THE BIRTH OF JESUS

The Bible: "Basic Instruction Before Leaving Earth" is a spiritual book and also a book of historical records. Being a book of historical records, the Bible has accurate accounts of key events with varying levels of detail. Hence, what records does the Bible have on the birth date and birthday celebration of our LORD and Savior, Jesus Christ? The Biblical Evidence will deal with the scriptural historical evidence for Christmas. In this chapter, we will examine the Bible records of Jesus' birth for the evidence of His birth date and birthday celebration. We will approach this in two ways: (1) the eyewitness accounts and (2) the prophetic revelation account.

1.1: The Eyewitness Accounts

There were many eyewitnesses to the birth, days, and ministry of Jesus Christ. His earthly parents, Mary and Joseph, the wise men, His disciples, the Gospel writers, etc. Why didn't someone deem it important to note and record the birth date of such a timeless great personage like Jesus Christ? Was it that the knowledge and act of dating events was not known? Could it be that God deliberately and carefully hid it from humanity? And if He did, what could have been the reason? Regarding the eyewitness account, we will consider the birth records of Jesus Christ in the Gospels of Luke and Matthew. These Bible books have detailed records of the birth of Jesus Christ. We want to carefully examine those details to see what they have on the date of Jesus' birth.

Luke 2:4-12

⁴And Joseph also went up from Galilee, out of the city of Nazareth, into Judaea, unto the city of David, which is called Bethlehem; (because he was of the house and lineage of David:) ⁵To be taxed with Mary his espoused wife, being great with child. ⁶And so it was, that, while they were there, the days were accomplished that she should be delivered. ⁷And she brought forth her firstborn son, and wrapped him in swaddling clothes, and laid him in a manger; because there was no room for them in the inn. ⁸And there were in the same country shepherds abiding in the field, keeping watch over their flock by night. And, lo, the angel of the Lord came upon them, and the glory of the Lord shone round about them: and they were sore afraid. ¹⁰ And the angel said unto them, Fear not: for, behold, I bring you good tidings of great joy, which shall be to all people. ¹¹For unto you is born this day in the city of David a Saviour, which is Christ the Lord. ¹²And this shall be a sign unto you; Ye shall find the babe wrapped in swaddling clothes, lying in a manger.

Verse 11 of Luke chapter 2 specified the day that Jesus was born. Luke 2:11, *"For unto you is born this day in the city of David a Saviour, which is Christ the Lord."* And which day is it? This day. This day could be any day. It could have been January 1st, or any other day of the twelve months. The specific day, month, or year of His birth was not given. The Word of God simply states in the book of Luke that Jesus the Savior, was born this day. Now let's examine the record of Jesus' birth in the book of Mathew and see what it says.

Matthew 1:23-25

23Behold, a virgin shall be with child, and shall bring forth a son, and they shall call his name Emmanuel, which being interpreted is, God with us. 24Then Joseph being raised from sleep did as the angel of the Lord had bidden him, and took unto him his wife: 25And knew her not till she had brought forth her firstborn son: and he called his name Jesus.

Matthew 2:1-2

2Now when Jesus was born in Bethlehem of Judaea in the days of Herod the king, behold, there came wise men from the east to Jerusalem, 2Saying, Where is he that is born King of the Jews? for we have seen his star in the east, and are come to worship him.

The record of Jesus' birth in Matthew also does not have the specific date of His birth. Its record did not specify the day, month, or year of His birth. The books of Matthew and Luke are the only two of the four Gospels that give an account of the birth of Jesus Christ. However, they did not account for the day, month, or year of Jesus' birth. The Bible gives no record of the date of Jesus' birth. Was this just an inadvertent omission, or was it a deliberate one? Definitely, it was not an unintended omission, but an intentional, purposeful omission. This is true because date recording has been in use long before the birth of Jesus. Right

11

from Genesis, the Bible has recorded precise dates of events. Even events that the writer was not present at the time of their occurrence. The Old Testament's dated accounts of events demonstrate that the knowledge of, and the use of date recording, had long existed before the days of Jesus Christ.

Genesis 7:11

In the six hundredth year of Noah's life, in the second month, the seventeenth day of the month, the same day were all the fountains of the great deep broken up, and the windows of heaven were opened.

Genesis 8:4-5

⁴And the ark rested in the seventh month, on the seventeenth day of the month, upon the mountains of Ararat. ⁵And the waters decreased continually until the tenth month: in the tenth month, on the first day of the month, were the tops of the mountains seen.

Genesis 8:13-14

¹³And it came to pass in the six hundredth and first year, in the first month, the first day of the month, the waters were dried up from off the earth: and Noah removed the covering of the ark, and looked, and, behold, the face of the ground was dry.¹⁴And in the second month, on the seven and twentieth day of the month, was the earth dried.

If we examine verse fourteen of Genesis chapter eight, we can tell the exact day and month that the earth dried. Which is the twenty-seventh day of the second month, that is, February 27. God revealed to Moses the knowledge about the creation and destruction of the first world. God revealed to him the details

12

about the years, months, and days of events as recorded in Genesis 7:11, Genesis 8:4-5, and Genesis 8:13-14. Therefore, through God's revelation, Moses received accurate details of the dates of events that occurred perhaps thousands of years before. This fact proves God's willingness and ability to reveal dates of events to His prophets. It is also evident that the knowledge of dating events already existed and was in use long before the birth of Jesus.

Furthermore, months were not only known by their numerical order, as mentioned earlier in Genesis, but were also known by names. The biblical records for dates were not as simple as "in the seventh month, in the second month, or in the tenth month," but they were also known by names before the birth of Jesus. Here are some biblical accounts for the names of months.

Exodus 34:18

The feast of unleavened bread shalt thou keep. Seven days thou shalt eat unleavened bread, as I commanded thee, in the time of the month Abib: for in the month Abib thou camest out from Egypt.

1 Kings 6:1

And it came to pass in the four hundred and eightieth year after the children of Israel were come out of the land of Egypt, in the fourth year of Solomon's reign over Israel, in the month Zif, which is the second month, that he began to build the house of the LORD.

Esther 3:7

In the first month, that is, the month Nisan, in the twelfth year of king Ahasuerus, they cast Pur, that is, the lot, before Haman from day to day, and from month to month, to the twelfth month, that is, the month Adar.

Esther 8:9

Then were the king's scribes called at that time in the third month, that is, the month Sivan, on the three and twentieth day thereof; ...

Esther 9:17

On the thirteenth day of the month Adar; and on the fourteenth day of the same rested they, and made it a day of feasting and gladness.

These Old Testament Bible verses also used the names of the months in their accounts for events. These verses name four months in their accounts of events: Abib, Zif, Nisan, and Adar. This proves that there was a perfect knowledge of, and the practice of, dating events long before Jesus was born. The Gospel writers were knowledgeable in the use of dates and were eyewitnesses to Jesus' days and ministry. However, they did not record the date of Jesus' birth. They did not know the date and were not inspired to add it to the Gospels. Mary, the mother of Jesus, was with them, and if God wanted the birthday of Jesus to be known. He would have inspired them to ask Mary, or He would have revealed it to them. This fact proves that God did not want humanity to know the date of Jesus' birth. Also, in the Old Testament, God gave prophecies about the birth of Jesus Christ with precise accuracy and details, without giving the year, month, or day of his birth. Definitely, the omission of Jesus' birth date in the Gospels was not an unintended omission, but an intentional, purposeful omission. The question is, why did God hide it from humanity?

1.2: The Prophetic Revelation Accounts

God revealed the birth of Jesus Christ to Prophet Isaiah and other Prophets with precise accuracy and details. Nonetheless, no biblical prophecy about Jesus revealed the birth date of Jesus Christ. God did not reveal the actual day, month, or year of Jesus's birth to any of the prophets. Could this also have been an unintended omission or a deliberate one? Or is it that God could not reveal dates of past and future events? Absolutely not, God revealed to Moses the precise date that the flood dried up from the earth. Genesis 8:13-14, *"¹³And it came to pass in the six hundredth and first year, in the first month, the first day of the month, the waters were dried up from off the earth: and Noah removed the covering of the ark, and looked, and, behold, the face of the ground was dry.¹⁴And in the second month, on the seven and twentieth day of the month, was the earth dried."* God revealed these precise dates of events regarding Noah and the flood to Moses. However, Prophet Isaiah received from God the most profound prophetic revelation on Jesus' birth with precise and accurate details, but His birth date was not revealed.

Isaiah 9:6-7

⁶For unto us a child is born, unto us a son is given: and the government shall be upon his shoulder: and his name shall be called Wonderful, Counsellor, The mighty God, The everlasting Father, The Prince of Peace. ⁷Of the increase of his government and peace there shall be no end, upon the throne of David, and upon his kingdom, to order it, and to establish it with judgment and with justice from henceforth even for ever. The zeal of the Lord of hosts will perform this.

Isaiah 53:2-10

²For he shall grow up before him as a tender plant, and as a root out of a dry ground: he hath no form nor comeliness; and when we shall see him, there is no beauty that we should desire him. ³He is despised and rejected of men; a man of sorrows, and acquainted with grief: and we hid as it were our faces from him; he was despised, and we esteemed him not. ⁴Surely he hath borne our griefs, and carried our sorrows: yet we did esteem him stricken, smitten of God, and afflicted. ⁵But he was wounded for our transgressions, he was bruised for our iniquities: the chastisement of our peace was upon him; and with his stripes we are healed. ⁶All we like sheep have gone astray; we have turned every one to his own way; and the Lord hath laid on him the iniquity of us all. ⁷He was oppressed, and he was afflicted, yet he opened not his mouth: he is brought as a lamb to the slaughter, and as a sheep before her shearers is dumb, so he openeth not his mouth. ⁸He was taken from prison and from judgment: and who shall declare his generation? for he was cut off out of the land of the living: for the transgression of my people was he stricken. ⁹And he made his grave with the wicked, and with the rich in his death; because he had done no violence, neither was any deceit in his mouth. ¹⁰Yet it pleased the Lord to bruise him; he hath put him to grief: when thou shalt make his soul an offering for sin, he shall see his seed, he shall prolong his days, and the pleasure of the Lord shall prosper in his hand. 11 He shall see of the travail of his soul, and shall be satisfied: by his knowledge shall my righteous servant justify many; for he shall bear their iniquities. 12 Therefore will I divide him a portion with the great, and he shall divide the spoil with the strong; because he hath poured out his soul unto death: and he was numbered with the transgressors; and he bare the sin of many, and made intercession for the transgressors.

In Isaiah's prophecies, we can see the accurate details of Jesus' life, including his suffering, death, the purpose of his coming, His continual reign for all eternity, and his intercessory role for the saints. God gave these accurate details about Jesus, yet He deliberately did not give His birth month or a birth date. All Bible prophecies about Jesus were precise in detail and were all fulfilled. Here are a few more references for biblical prophecies about Jesus:

Deuteronomy 18:18-19

[18]I will raise them up a Prophet from among their brethren, like unto thee, and will put my words in his mouth; and he shall speak unto them all that I shall command him. 19 And it shall come to pass, that whosoever will not hearken unto my words which he shall speak in my name, I will require it of him.

Micah 5:2

2 But thou, Bethlehem Ephratah, though thou be little among the thousands of Judah, yet out of thee shall he come forth unto me that is to be ruler in Israel; whose goings forth have been from of old, from everlasting.

Although the knowledge and act of date recording were taught and used in the days of these prophets. And God, being

17

capable of revealing accurate dates of events to his prophets, as evidenced in His revealing of dates of past events to Moses. Nonetheless, God deliberately chose not to reveal the birth date of Christ to the prophet Isaiah and others. The time difference between Isaiah and Moses amounts to about 750 years. Isaiah started his prophetic ministry around 755 BC, while Moses received the Ten Commandments at Mount Sinai around 1445 BC. In the time of Moses, the use of date recording with the month's name was already in use. God revealed to Moses the accurate dates for events that happened many years before his time. Could He not have done the same many years later in His revelation of Jesus' birth to Isaiah? God revealed accurate details about Jesus' birth and ministry to Prophet Isaiah. Could He not have given Isaiah the date of Jesus' birth? Yes, God was able to do so, but He purposefully omitted Jesus' date of birth in His revelations. The question we should be asking as Christians is, why did He not reveal it?

Deuteronomy 29:29

The secret things belong unto the LORD our God: but those things which are revealed belong unto us and to our children for ever, that we may do all the words of this law.

CHAPTER 2

THE IMPORTANCE ATTRIBUTED TO JESUS' BIRTHDAY IN THE BIBLE

Christians, as followers of Jesus, must examine the importance the Bible attributed to Jesus' birthday. The Bible, being the Ultimate Source of Authority, must be the only reference point for all Christian truth and practices. To accurately follow the footsteps of Jesus, it's imperative to know the importance Jesus and the Apostles attributed to His birthday. Apostle Paul was very mindful of this and implored Christians to follow him only as he follows Christ. 1 Corinthians 11:1, *"Be ye followers of me, even as I also am of Christ."* Therefore, Christianity and its practices must follow the pattern that Christ has laid. Christians should never follow any leader outside the footprint of Jesus Christ. That was what Apostle Paul was saying to his followers in 1 Corinthians 11:1.

2.1: The Importance Jesus Attributed To His Birthday

What weight did Jesus give to his birthday? Jesus did not reveal His birthday to His disciples while on earth, nor did He reveal it to them through prophecy after His departure. Throughout His ministry on earth, Jesus never talked about His birth. Obviously, Jesus did not attribute any importance to His birthday. The question is, why did God not reveal Jesus' birth date to the Prophets, and why did Jesus not reveal it to His disciples? God did not reveal Jesus' birthday because He deemed it unprofitable and unnecessary for our Christian faith and holiness. Jesus did not reveal His birthday, nor celebrate it, because it was unprofitable for our Christian journey and eternal life. However, the Bible reveals an event that Jesus deemed profitable and necessary for our Christian journey, holiness, and eternal life. The same did Jesus command Christians to observe often, without attaching a date to it

Luke 22:18-20

[18] For I say unto you, I will not drink of the fruit of the vine, until the kingdom of God shall come. [19] And he took bread, and gave thanks, and brake it, and gave unto them, saying, This is my body which is given for you: this do in remembrance of me. [20] Likewise also the cup after supper, saying, This cup is the new testament in my blood, which is shed for you.

1 Corinthians 11:23-26

[23] For I have received of the Lord that which also I delivered unto you, that the Lord Jesus the same night in which he was betrayed took bread: [24] And when he had given thanks,

*he brake it, and said, Take, eat: this is my body, which is broken for you: this do in remembrance of me. *[25]*After the same manner also he took the cup, when he had supped, saying, this cup is the new testament in my blood: this do ye, as oft as ye drink it, in remembrance of me. *[26]*For as often as ye eat this bread, and drink this cup, ye do shew the Lord's death till he come.*

Knowing the corruption that would result from attaching a date to remembering His death, Jesus commanded that it be done often without glorifying a day. Jesus had communion with his disciples. He broke bread after giving thanks, He gave them to eat, and likewise the wine He gave them to drink. Then, He commanded them to do the same in remembrance of Him. The disciples observed the same, as the LORD commanded, without attributing a date to it. If Jesus' birthday was necessary for the Christian faith, holiness, and eternal life. He would have commanded His disciples to observe it without attaching a date to it, like He did for His death and resurrection.

In Luke 22:18-20 above, Jesus gives one of his last instructions, if not his last instruction, before his death. When a father is departing, or leaving for a journey, he gives instructions to his children or family on the most important things to be done. Similarly, Jesus instructed His disciples before His death and departure on things that are important and beneficial. He said, "Do this in remembrance of me", and often, without attaching a particular day to it. Therefore, Christians could do it monthly, quarterly, or even weekly, as often as they are able to do it in remembrance of Him. This is the Holy Communion (Eucharist) that the churches observe in remembrance of Jesus' death for the sins of humanity. Some churches do it monthly, some quarterly, and some weekly. This is not the Easter celebration; Jesus did not ordain that, but man, and it breeds corruption. Jesus did not attribute importance to His birth, but to His death. He only commanded His followers to observe the LORD's Supper (Eucharist) as often as possible in remembrance of His death. Jesus carefully commanded that it be done as frequently as possible to prevent His followers from corrupting themselves by glorifying a day for celebration. The Apostles understood Jesus' commandment on the Lord's Supper. They walked not in the flesh, but in the spirit. They focused on the essence of the commandment, which is observing a solemn rite to remember Jesus' sacrificial death for sin as often as possible.

1 Corinthians 11:23-26

[23] For I have received of the Lord that which also I delivered unto you, that the Lord Jesus the same night in which he was betrayed took bread: [24] And when he had given thanks, he brake it, and said, Take, eat: this is my body, which is broken for you: this do in remembrance of me. [25] After the same manner also he took the cup, when he had supped, saying, this cup is the new testament in my blood: this do ye, as oft as ye drink it, in remembrance of me. [26] For as often as ye eat this bread, and drink this cup, ye do shew the Lord's death till he come.

Paul said that he also received from the LORD the instructions He gave on the night He was betrayed, pointing to Luke 22:18-20. Apostle Paul was not present the night Jesus instructed His disciples to observe the LORD's Supper. Nonetheless, through divine revelation, Jesus also instructed him to observe it. 1 Corinthians 11:23, *"For I have received of the Lord that which also I delivered unto you, that the Lord*

Jesus the same night in which he was betrayed took bread:"
God does not do things carelessly or randomly; He is a God of purpose and a God of order. God has a good reason for not giving attention to Jesus' birthday, and you will find out as we read on. However, we can see the disciples practicing exactly what the LORD commanded them, as Apostle Paul referenced. Paul gave his followers the Eucharist as the LORD had given it to His disciples and commanded to be observed. The commandment that Jesus gave was to focus on His death, and He asked us, His disciples, to do this in remembrance of him, NOT His birthday. This reveals that Jesus did not attach any significance to his birthday in Christianity. He never mentioned His birthday, never celebrated it, and never asked His disciples to celebrate or commemorate His birthday. If remembering or celebrating His birthday was necessary for the Christian journey and holiness, He would have commanded it to be done. Jesus only commanded Christians to remember His death often (Holy Communion) without attaching a date, like they have done with Easter. He did not command anyone to remember His birthday or celebrate a day called Christmas.

2.2: The Importance The Apostles Gave To Jesus' Birthday

After Jesus departed, the Apostles were given charge of the gospel, as we are in charge now after they have departed. Christians are to continue the same Christianity that the Apostles took over from Jesus. Therefore, it's imperative to understand the importance the Apostles attributed to the birthday of Jesus Christ. This will enable Christians today to recognize the importance we must also attribute to Jesus' birthday. The Apostles understood that God had deemed the birthdate of Jesus unnecessary for their faith, holiness, and eternal life because He never revealed it. They also observed that Jesus did not mention or celebrate His birthday because He deemed it unnecessary and unprofitable for their Christian life and holiness. Therefore, the Apostles paid no attention to Jesus' birthday nor celebrate it. Throughout the Apostles' teachings, we can see that they gave no attention to Jesus' birth, but emphasized His death and resurrection as the significant event of the Christian faith. Apostle Paul categorically said that if Christ has not risen, then the gospel and the Christian faith are vain. 1 Corinthians 15:14, *"And if Christ be not risen, then is our preaching vain, and your faith is also vain."*

Therefore, Christianity centers and focuses on Christ's death. It is for this reason that Jesus commanded Christians to remember His death by observing the Holy Communion without attaching a particular day or date to it. Although Christ's death is the core of salvation and Christianity, the Scripture does not provide the exact day of his death. This was intentionally done by God so that the date does not become the focus and corrupt the Christian faith. The book of Romans sheds light on how the Apostles emphasized the death and resurrection of Jesus Christ and gave no attention to His birth.

Romans 1:4-5

[4]And declared to be the Son of God with power, according to the spirit of holiness, by the resurrection from the dead: [5]By whom we have received grace and apostleship, for obedience to the faith among all nations, for his name

The Bible is saying: The Son of God, with power according to the Spirit of holiness, by the resurrection from the dead, gave the Apostles the grace and apostleship. It is the power of the

24

Holy Spirit that resurrected Jesus from the dead, and through His resurrection, Paul and others were empowered to become Apostles and to obey God. It is through the belief in the death and resurrection of Jesus that people receive salvation and power for holiness. That is why the Bible said that without Christ's resurrection, the gospel and our faith are in vain. 1 Corinthians 15:14, *"And if Christ be not risen, then is our preaching vain, and your faith is also vain."* It is the death and resurrection of Christ that gave the apostles (and us) the grace to be Christians and the power to live holy.

Romans 6:4-5

⁴Therefore we are buried with him by baptism into death: that like as Christ was raised up from the dead by the glory of the Father, even so we also should walk in newness of life. ⁵For if we have been planted together in the likeness of his death, we shall be also in the likeness of his resurrection:

Note that the emphasis again is on Jesus' death. We are baptized into his death, and shall also be in the likeness of his resurrection. That as Christ was raised from the dead by the glory of the Father, even so we should walk in the newness of life. The Apostle focused on Christ's death and resurrection as the core of the Christian faith. It is Christ's death and resurrection that empower people to become Christians and to live holy. The Apostles focused on the death and resurrection of Christ because that was what Jesus taught them. He commanded them to focus on his death and remember it often. Jesus did not attribute any importance to His birth; the Apostles understood this. Therefore, they neither spoke about Jesus' birthday nor celebrated it at any point in time in their ministry.

CHAPTER 3

THE ESSENCE OF CHRISTIANITY

Everlasting life is the essence of Christianity. Jesus came and died on the cross to save those who would believe and grant them eternal life. Christianity is not about eating, drinking, and celebrating. It's not even about healing, deliverance, prosperity, and breakthroughs. Jesus came and died for nothing else but to save humanity from the power of sin and its wages. That those who believe in Him should not perish but have eternal life. Therefore, the gospel of Jesus Christ is to bring salvation to sinners that they may have everlasting life.

John 3:16-19

¹⁶For God so loved the world, that he gave his only begotten Son, that whosoever believeth in him should not perish, but have everlasting life. ¹⁷For God sent not his Son into the world to condemn the world; but that the world through him might be saved. ¹⁸He that believeth on him is not condemned: but he that believeth not is condemned already, because he hath not believed in the name of the only begotten Son of God. ¹⁹And this is the condemnation, that light is come into the world, and men loved darkness rather than light, because their deeds were evil.

Romans 6:23

For the wages of sin is death; but the gift of God is eternal life through Jesus Christ our Lord.

Jesus' mission on earth was to save humanity from their sin and its wages, and grant them eternal life. His mission is evident through His teachings and ultimately His death on the cross. His disciples understood His mission and the gospel His death and resurrection brought to humanity. The Gospel means "good news." The good news that Jesus' death and resurrection brought is the forgiveness of sin and eternal life. Therefore, His disciples went about preaching the gospel of Jesus Christ that humanity might have everlasting life. If Jesus' birthday celebration is necessary for salvation and eternal life, then it would reflect in the gospel they preached.

3.1: The Gospel Of Jesus Christ:

The aim of the gospel of Jesus Christ is eternal life. The Christian journey is that of holiness unto everlasting life. Therefore, the gospel of Jesus Christ is centered on matters and principles that facilitate attaining eternal life. If the celebration of Jesus' birthday is necessary for salvation and eternal life, then it would reflect in the gospel. A sample of the gospel preached by Apostle Paul and Peter will give insight into the gospel that the Apostles preached.

1 Corinthians 15:1-4

[15]Moreover, brethren, I declare unto you the gospel which I preached unto you, which also ye have received, and wherein ye stand; [2]By which also ye are saved, if ye keep in

memory what I preached unto you, unless ye have believed in vain. ³For I delivered unto you first of all that which I also received, how that Christ died for our sins according to the scriptures; ⁴And that he was buried, and that he rose again the third day according to the scriptures:

The above is the gospel that Apostle Paul said he preached, the death and resurrection of Jesus Christ. He said it was this gospel which they received from him that saved them and made them to stand in the faith. He also said that it was the same gospel he received. Now, below is the gospel Apostle Peter preached to the crowd of people who gathered after witnessing the events that took place after Pentecost. That is, after Jesus' disciples were baptized with the Holy Ghost, evidenced by speaking in tongues.

Acts 2:14,22-24,29-33,36-37

¹⁴But Peter, standing up with the eleven, lifted up his voice, and said unto them, Ye men of Judaea, and all ye that dwell at Jerusalem, be this known unto you, and hearken to my words: ²²Ye men of Israel, hear these words; Jesus of Nazareth, a man approved of God among you by miracles and wonders and signs, which God did by him in the midst of you, as ye yourselves also know: ²³Him, being delivered by the determinate counsel and foreknowledge of God, ye have taken, and by wicked hands have crucified and slain: ²⁴Whom God hath raised up, having loosed the pains of death: because it was not possible that he should be holden of it. ²⁹Men and brethren, let me freely speak unto you of the patriarch David, that he is both dead and buried, and his sepulchre is with us unto this day. ³⁰Therefore being a prophet, and knowing that God had sworn with an oath to him, that of the fruit of his loins, according to the flesh, he would raise up Christ to sit on his throne; [31]He seeing this before spake of the resurrection of Christ, that his soul was not left in hell, neither his flesh did see corruption. [32]This Jesus hath God raised up, whereof we all are witnesses. [33]Therefore being by the right hand of God exalted, and having received of the Father the promise of the Holy Ghost, he hath shed forth this, which ye now see and hear. [36]Therefore let all the house of Israel know assuredly, that God hath made that same Jesus, whom ye have crucified, both Lord and Christ. [37]Now when they heard this, they were pricked in their heart, and said unto Peter and to the rest of the apostles, Men and brethren, what shall we do? [38]Then Peter said unto them, Repent, and be baptized every one of you in the name of Jesus Christ for the remission of sins, and ye shall receive the gift of the Holy Ghost.

The gospel of our Lord Jesus Christ is built on His death and resurrection as narrated by the Apostles Paul and Peter. Christians are buried together with Christ in baptism in the likeness of His death and will be resurrected in the likeness of His resurrection. What brought Christians into covenant with God is the death and resurrection of Jesus. We shall also be resurrected into glory for eternity in the likeness of his resurrection. The focus of Paul's Christian journey was on the death and resurrection of Jesus Christ. He knew it was the core event of significance that mattered in the Christian faith. He gave no attention whatsoever to the birthday of Jesus Christ and did not celebrate it. He knew it was not necessary for his Christian faith, holiness, and eternal life.

Philippians 3:10-11

¹⁰That I may know him, and the power of his resurrection, and the fellowship of his sufferings, being made conformable unto his death; ¹¹If by any means I might attain unto the resurrection of the dead.

Apostle Paul's focus here is to know Jesus and the power of his resurrection so that he can conform to the death of Christ. He completely understood the gospel, that it's about the death and resurrection of Jesus Christ, and not about the baby Jesus. The gospel hangs on the death and the resurrection of Jesus Christ, not His birth. The Apostles understood this and focused on it. They were not distracted from the faith by the commemoration and celebration of the birth of Jesus Christ. Let us again examine what Apostle Peter has to say about this.

1 Peter 1:3-4

³Blessed be the God and Father of our Lord Jesus Christ, which according to his abundant mercy hath begotten us again unto a lively hope by the resurrection of Jesus Christ from the dead, ⁴To an inheritance incorruptible, and undefiled, and that fadeth not away, reserved in heaven for you,

This is the core of the gospel on which the Christian faith is built: the death and resurrection of Jesus. That is why Jesus commanded Christians to observe the Holy Communion often in remembrance of him. The Apostles stamped their feet on the death and resurrection of Jesus Christ, promoted it, focused on it, and often observed the Lord's Supper/Holy Communion. Through their writing, they ensured that the death and resurrection of Jesus took center stage in the hearts of believers.

The gospel the Apostle preached was focused on Jesus' suffering, death, and resurrection.

1 Corinthians 15:12-14

12Now if Christ be preached that he rose from the dead, how say some among you that there is no resurrection of the dead? 13But if there be no resurrection of the dead, then is Christ not risen: 14And if Christ be not risen, then is our preaching vain, and your faith is also vain

Can you see what the gospel and Christian faith are all about? Christ is preached, that he rose from the dead; that is what the gospel is about. The preaching of the suffering, the death, and the resurrection of Jesus Christ. That is the gospel, not the birth of a baby. Apostle Paul said, If what is being preached is the death and resurrection of Christ, and some say there is no resurrection. And if Christ did not resurrect, then the preaching of the gospel is vain and the Christian faith is also vain. This means that without the death and resurrection of Jesus Christ, the Christian faith is futile and profits nothing. It is evident that the Apostles strictly followed the footsteps of Jesus in preaching and practicing the gospel that He committed to their hands. The gospel was about preaching the death and resurrection of Jesus Christ; all the Apostles preached it. There is no biblical account of them preaching about the birth of Jesus or commemorating and celebrating His birthday. They all knew that according to the gospel that Jesus handed over to them, it was not necessary for their faith, holiness, and eternal life.

3.2: John 3:16 Christmas Relevance

Christians often quote John 3:16 to validate their Christmas Day celebration. They claim to be celebrating the gift of God to the world, referring to the child Jesus. John 3:16, *"For God so loved the world, that he gave his only begotten Son, that whosoever believeth in him should not perish, but have everlasting life."*

However, they fail to realize that what God gave is His Son and not His child. The giving is not referring to the birth of Jesus; God did not give the world a child, He gave a Son. The giving is in reference to the death of Jesus for the remission of sins. This understanding is consistent with the gospel that the Apostle preached. People misinterpret John 3:16 to support the Christmas celebration because they use it as a standalone verse. The Bible says that no scripture stands alone and none is of a private interpretation. Isaiah 34:16, *"Seek ye out of the book of the LORD, and read: no one of these shall fail, none shall want her mate: for my mouth it hath commanded, and his spirit it hath gathered them."* 2 Peter 1:20 *"Knowing this first, that no prophecy of the scripture is of any private interpretation."*

According to 2 Peter 1:20, the first thing to know when interpreting a scripture is that no one has a private interpretation. Isaiah 34:16 says that no scripture will fail to be fulfilled and none shall lack its mate, i.e., to provide a clear understanding of what the scripture is actually saying. And that the Spirit of God had gathered the mates of every word that God had spoken. Therefore, to better understand what John 3:16 is actually saying, we must find its mate. And one of its mates can be found in the book of Isaiah.

Isaiah 9:6

For unto us a child is born, unto us a son is given: and the government shall be upon his shoulder: and his name shall be called Wonderful, Counsellor, The mighty God, The everlasting Father, The Prince of Peace.

Isaiah 9:6 gives a clear distinction between the child and the son. It gives clarity to who was given, *"For unto us a child is born, unto us a son is given:"* Therefore, this scripture mate brings perfect understanding to what John 3:16 is actually saying: *"For God so loved the world, that he gave his only begotten Son* (died on the cross for the sins of the world), *that whosoever believeth in him should not perish, but have everlasting life."* God's Son was given "killed" on the cross, and not His baby or His child. God's child was born to us, BUT His Son was given to us. The giving is the death of Jesus Christ. That love of God to the world was centered on the death of Jesus Christ on the cross. For God so loved the world that he gave his son to be killed on the cross, that whosoever believes in him should not perish but have everlasting life. That is what that scripture is saying, and it is consistent with the gospel the Apostles received and preached. Romans 5:8, *"But God commendeth his love toward us, in that, while we were yet sinners, Christ died for us."*

For God so loved the world that he gave his only begotten Son: Christ died for us. God commended, that is, God showed or demonstrated His love towards us, in that while we were still sinners, we did not love Him; yet Christ died for us. That is the love of God, not the birth of a baby. The Apostles understood, as seen in the gospel that they believed and preached. There is no scriptural record of them speaking about or focusing on the birth of Jesus. Neither did they commemorate nor celebrate Jesus' birthday. The gospel they preached was solely on Christ's death and resurrection as a propitiation for sin and the gift of eternal life. Jesus himself did not speak about his birth. He did not reveal His birthday, He paid no attention to it, and did not celebrate it. Bearing in mind that the Bible is our USA "Ultimate Source of Authority," Should a heavenly-minded Christian not strictly adhere to it like the Apostle did? Should a true Christian not believe and order their life only by what the Bible says? Should they not stop where the Bible stopped? 2 Timothy 3:16, *"All scripture is given by inspiration of God, and is profitable for doctrine, for reproof, for correction, for instruction in righteousness:"*

3.3: Claims For The Month Of Jesus's Birth

Although the world is filled with resources for the evidence of how pagan practices metamorphosed into Christmas, through the Catholic Church. And eventually made their way to the Protestant mainstream Christianity. Nonetheless, I will not reference any extrabiblical sources for the pagan origin of the Christmas celebration. This does not mean that the sources and their claims are not credible. But because I want to focus solely on referencing the Bible, the Ultimate Source of Authority for truth. The Bible remains the ultimate guide to truth for serious Christians. Any information or resource about the origins of Christmas must agree with the Bible, because it's the Ultimate Source of Authority for truth. The Bible has the following records on the birth date of Jesus Christ:

(1) There are no records of God's revelation of the date of Jesus' birth.

(2) Jesus, throughout his earthly ministry, neither disclosed His birth date nor spoke of it, nor celebrated it.

(3) Jesus did not reveal His birth date to His disciples after ascending into heaven.

(4) The Apostles and early Christians never commemorated and celebrated Jesus' birthday as observed in the Scripture.

(5) Jesus never commanded Christians to observe His birthday; He commanded that we should observe the LORD's Supper often in remembrance of His death.

The Bible is the Ultimate Source of Authority for reference to truth in the Christian faith. It has no record of the birth of Jesus Christ, nor its celebrations, nor the command to celebrate it. Therefore, the December 25th Christmas Day celebration is an extrabiblical Christian faith practice. It has no biblical basis and is a nonbiblical Christian practice. Some people have attempted to arrive at the month of Jesus' birth by calculating from the month the angel Gabriel visited Mary. The book of Luke recorded the account of events and circumstances leading up to the birth of Jesus, which they have used for their calculation.

Luke 1:26-27, 31

26And in the sixth month the angel Gabriel was sent from God unto a city of Galilee, named Nazareth, 27To a virgin espoused to a man whose name was Joseph, of the house of David; and the virgin's name was Mary. 31And, behold, thou shalt conceive in thy womb, and bring forth a son, and shalt call his name Jesus.

The book of Luke says that the angel Gabriel came to Mary in the sixth month. Luke 1:26, *"And in the sixth month the*

Christmas!

angel Gabriel was sent from God unto a city of Galilee, named Nazareth, " This is important because some people have been erroneously misled into calculations of when Jesus was conceived. They calculate from the sixth month, say, June, then count nine months to March and believe that Jesus was born in March or April. But what was the message the angel Gabriel gave to Mary? Luke 1:3, *"And, behold, thou shalt conceive in thy womb, and bring forth a son, and shalt call his name Jesus."*

The angel did not tell Mary that she had already conceived. He did not tell her that she would conceive this month. He told her that she would conceive and call his name Jesus. He did not specify the month or the time period of her conception. Whether it was immediately, after a month, two months, six months, or more, it's not revealed. Then, when did she conceive? It's unknown and unknowable, and God wanted it so. The message that angel Gabriel gave to Mary is, "You shall conceive." God had carefully concealed the date and the time period in which it would happen. God intentionally concealed this knowledge so no one could claim to know the day or month of Jesus' birth. Therefore, any claim to have known the month of Jesus' birth is false. God concealed the day and month of Jesus' birth because it is unnecessary and unprofitable for the Christian faith, holiness, and eternal life.

Now, if you should examine the empirical evidence in your history on the December 25th Christmas celebration. That is, from the day you were born to this day, you would understand why Jesus never revealed His birthday. And neither celebrated it nor commanded His followers to celebrate it. Judging from your experience of the way the Christmas season is portrayed, promoted, and celebrated. Would you say that Jesus Christ is the reason for the season? From your observations from the time you learned of the celebration of Christmas to date. The things you have observed, heard, and been part of, could you conclude that Jesus is really the reason for the season? Let's examine the empirical evidence for the Christmas celebration.

Part 2

THE EMPIRICAL

EVIDENCE

CHAPTER 4

THE SECULAR WORLD EVIDENCE

Empirical evidence here deals with the facts or knowledge acquired through experience and observation without using scientific methods or theory. You don't have to be a scientist; it's just about your observations and experiences. A layman can put together such evidence about anything because it is all about what they have seen and experienced. Empirical evidence is about observations and experiences rather than theories. Therefore, we are not concerned with what was written or reported in time past. It's not about what someone taught you or some scientific theory. Rather, we want to validate what the Bible says through our observations and experiences of Christmas celebrations. We are considering my observation and experiences, yours, and those of others. And without a shadow of doubt, these observations and experiences speak louder than words.

In Part One: "The Biblical Evidence," we dealt with scriptural historical evidence for Christmas. We examined Bible records of Jesus' birth for evidence of His birth date and birthday celebration. Since the Bible is the Ultimate Source of Authority for truth in Christianity. We examined the historical scriptural records to uncover the truth about the birth date and birthday celebration of Jesus Christ. To understand the basis for, and the relevance of, the December 25th Christmas celebration in Christianity. The careful examination of biblical records revealed no evidence for the December 25th Christmas celebration or for any other day. The only logical conclusion that could be drawn from the biblical records is that God deliberately withheld revealing the birth date of Jesus. And because it was unprofitable for the Christian faith, holiness, and eternal life.

Now, let's examine the empirical evidence in our contemporary history on the December 25th Christmas celebration. That is, the observable evidence in our lifetime to understand why Jesus never revealed His birthday. Neither celebrated it nor commanded His followers to celebrate it. If we examine what we have observed and experienced about the ways the Christmas season is portrayed, promoted, and celebrated. Can we say that Jesus Christ is the reason for the season? Based on your observations and experiences since the time you learned of the celebration of Christmas to date. The things you have observed, heard, and experienced, could you conclude that Jesus is really the reason for the season? The first empirical evidence to be considered is the secular world. The secular world holds a lot of irrefutable empirical evidence for why Jesus never revealed His birthday nor commanded Christians to celebrate or commemorate it.

4.1: God's Word On The Secular World

The word secular relates to worldly things; things and people not associated with spirituality or the Holy God. The secular world is the worldly people, i.e., those who only want to gratify self and

The Empirical Evidence

flesh, and treat themselves to pleasure. Those who care only about the things of this world and its pleasures. Whose priorities and concerns only relate to this secular world and life. But before we examine the secular world evidence. It's imperative to see what the Bible says about the secular world. Although the focus is on the empirical evidence from the secular world. Nonetheless, to understand the secular world's empirical evidence for Christmas, we must understand what God says about it.

Romans 8:5-7

5For they that are after the flesh do mind the things of the flesh; but they that are after the Spirit the things of the Spirit 6For to be carnally minded is death; but to be spiritually minded is life and peace 7Because the carnal mind is enmity against God: for it is not subject to the law of God, neither indeed can be.

God said that the carnally minded are His enemies. It is that bad! Their carnal mind is in enmity against God because it cannot be subject to God's law and will only lead them to death. Romans 8:6-7, *6For to be carnally minded is death;... 7Because the carnal mind is enmity against God: for it is not subject to the law of God, neither indeed can be.* The Bible says that being only concerned about secular living, and secular life is death. Why is it so? Because the carnal mind, the mind that is concerned with secular things, is in enmity with God. A carnally minded person is an enemy of God because their carnal mind cannot obey the law of God. According to God's Word, the person who is focused on gratifying this flesh, or just fulfilling life in this world alone, is an enemy of God. They are an enemy of God because they do not have God in their heart, and do not think about or do what is right with God. That is what God says about the secular world, the secular people, the worldly people, the fleshly people, the carnal people. God says they are his enemy because of their carnal mindset that cannot obey His law.

God further warns Christians that friendship with worldly people is enmity with Him. That is, relating intimately with worldly people for ungodly outcomes is enmity with God. Who are your friends? What do you do with your friends? It is said, Show me your friends and I will tell you who you are. If your friends are worldly people. Then you are people of like minds, "carnally minded." Birds of the same feather flock together. You move together, you agree on the same things, you have the same passion, you have the same goal, you enjoy the same things. Hence, friendship with the world, that is, carnally minded people, makes you carnally minded and turns you into an enemy of God. Therefore, whatsoever the world loves and enjoys should alert a heavenly-minded Christian to pause, think, and examine carefully before getting involved.

James 4:4

Ye adulterers and adulteresses, know ye not that the friendship of the world is enmity with God? whosoever therefore will be a friend of the world is the enemy of God.

Once a Christian turns to the secular way of living, they become an enemy of God. Once your mind begins to reason like worldly people and accepts their ways of life and their standards, you are no longer a Christian. If you are friends with the world, God says you are His enemy. God's standard is clearly firm and consequential. So, if you choose the way of the world, the way they live, the way they do things, the way they reason, the things that give them pleasure, God says you will become his enemy.

Remember that whatsoever the world loves should always alert a heavenly-minded Christian to pause, think, and examine carefully before getting involved. Whatever interests the world, whatever the world loves and engages in, should always be a trigger to a heavenly-minded Christian to pause and think. And say, Hey! Wait a minute, the world loves this so much, how come? Think about it, do your research, and know whether it is something you should be part of or not, so you don't become worldly and God's enemy. With this foundational knowledge and understanding, let us explore the observable evidence for Christmas in the secular world. Let's empirically verify whether Jesus is really the reason for the December 25th Christmas celebration.

4.2: The Secular People's Love For Christmas

Let's examine the empirical evidence from secular people in the world, atheists, people of other religions like Muslims, Hindus, Buddhists, etc. People who do not believe in Jesus Christ, who died for the salvation of the world. The secular world also includes nominal Christians, that is, Christians by name only. People who are mainly Christians by birth or affiliation. People who may have been born into a family that attended church, or born in a nation that professes or accepts Christianity. Christians who may have been born again at one point but have backslidden into the world, but still identify as Christians. Everyone in the secular world has one thing in common: they despise the laws of God and do not obey Jesus, including the nominal Christians. Luke 6:46, *"And why call ye me, Lord, Lord, and do not the things which I say?"* They are all carnally minded and therefore in enmity with God, but they love Christmas! Romans 8:6-7, *⁶For to be carnally minded is death;... ⁷Because the carnal mind*

*is enmity against God: for it is not subject to the law of God,
neither indeed can be.*

These people who do not believe in Jesus, who is supposedly
the reason for the season, love Christmas? The secular world,
whose carnal minds are not subject to the law of God, loves to
partake in Christmas traditions like everyone else. Some of them
outrightly hate Jesus, but they love the Christmas celebrations
and participate in them. These individuals do not want to be
bothered with the gospel. Nominal Christians who do not care
about God's laws and are unresponsive to the gospel truth for
eternal life. Preach Jesus to them, and they are irritated and
offended at the gospel of Jesus, whom they claim to know and
believe in. In fact, they hate Jesus and want nothing to do with
him besides the casual mentioning of His name during Christmas,
Easter, and a few other days in the year. Yet most, if not all, enjoy
and participate in the Christmas celebration in one way or
another; they have no problem with it. They hate Jesus, but they
love Christmas! And yet you say, Jesus is the reason for the
season? The empirical evidence for secular people's love and
participation in the December 25th Christmas season celebration
is evident to all.

I once had a co-worker who was an enemy of the Christian
faith. He identifies as a Christian, a nominal Christian that is. I
will leave his name unmentioned. His views oppose the Christian
faith. He castigates all pastors and churches regardless of their
righteousness, and is against everything about Christianity. He
castigates Jesus, saying that He is a white man. He castigates the
Bible, saying that it's just man's writing. He hates everything
about Jesus, the Word of God, and anything that has to do with
Christianity and the church. However, he is always the first

person to send me Christmas wishes, Christmas songs, and the like. He is not just sending them because he only wants to wish me Merry Christmas; no, not just that, he LOVES Christmas. Whenever I confront him on his conflicting hatred for Christianity and love for Christmas. He will respond, "There is nothing wrong with Christmas, so I have the right to enjoy it." This man loves Christmas but hates Jesus and the Word of God. And yet people say, Jesus is the reason for the season?

I also had another coworker, this time a Muslim, whose name I will also not mention. Muslims do not regard Jesus as the Son of God; to them, Jesus is just a prophet, and not God. They claim that Jesus did not die on the cross. This is the belief of my Muslim coworker. He was a practicing Muslim and wanted nothing to do with the gospel of Jesus and His commandments. This man wants nothing to do with Jesus or the Christian faith, but he loves Christmas more than anybody I have ever seen. Christmas drives him crazy for pleasure. He loves Christmas, yet he does not love Jesus Christ. He loves the song "Mr. Grinch" and mocks me with it because I don't celebrate Christmas. This practicing Muslim coworker of mine wants nothing to do with Jesus and Christianity. But he loves Christmas and always participates in the December 25th Christmas celebrations. And Christians say, Jesus is the reason for the season? The world loves Christmas a lot, but hates Jesus Christ. This should alarm a heavenly-minded Christian and anyone who desires truth.

The empirical evidence of secular people's love for Christmas celebration should trigger a heavenly-minded Christian to pause. Then, think, seek knowledge, and ask God about the Christmas celebration in prayers. Whatsoever the world loves should always alert a heavenly-minded Christian to pause, think, and examine carefully before getting involved. Whatever excites the carnally-minded person, whatsoever the world loves and engages in, should always be a trigger to a heavenly-minded Christian to pause and think. To avoid becoming carnally minded like the secular world, and invariably an enemy of God. It is much better to be called Mr. or Mrs. Grinch than to be in enmity with God.

4.3: The Secular Organizations' Love For Christmas

Let's examine the empirical evidence for the secular organizations' love for Christmas season celebrations. Most secular organizations prohibit Christians from preaching Jesus in any way in the workplace. This applies to both private and public workplaces, in the mainstream media, government/organizations, schools, and businesses. They restrict and stifle Christians and the Word of God in the workplace. They despise the name of Jesus and don't want prayers to be made in his name. They want nothing to do with Jesus; they hate Him, but have no problem celebrating Christmas. And yet, you say, Jesus is the reason for the season? They love the December 25th Christmas season celebrations. They decorate the workplace for the Christmas season, participate in and enjoy the celebration. They love the Christmas season because it's good for merchandising and profit. They have no problem with the Christmas celebrations, but hate Jesus and want nothing to do with Him. And yet, some Christians say, Jesus is the reason for the season. Now, let's examine what I have observed and experienced; my empirical evidence.

I worked at a retail store in Northshore Mall in Peabody, Massachusetts, when I came to the United States. It was my first job in the US. I will refrain from naming the business organization. During my orientation, I was informed that I am not allowed to preach the gospel of Jesus in the workplace. It was prohibited for me to discuss religion or discuss my faith in the workplace. I knew what I had to do, and did what Jesus required of me as a Christian. Of course, I respectfully discussed religion, and I preach the gospel of Jesus to everyone possible. They hate Jesus and want nothing to do with Him. They did not want me to talk about Jesus. However, once November arrives, they will decorate the store and start playing Christmas songs, such as "Jingle Bells" and "Rudolph the Red-Nosed Reindeer," among others. They will bring Christmas images to decorate the store, and wish people Merry Christmas. They celebrate and give customers Christmas discounts. They love Christmas for the sake of merchandising and profit. They love celebrating Christmas because it's good for business. They do not like the laws of God; they despise Jesus, hate Him, and want nothing to do with Him, but they LOVE Christmas. And you say, Jesus is the reason for the season? Whatever the secular world loves should always alarm a heavenly-minded Christian to pause, think, and pray about it before getting involved.

On my last day of work at this company. I believe it was the last Friday of February 2008. I was working and worshiping God with songs in my heart. Unexpectedly, I was startled by the voice of my supervisor, Carthy. I did not realize I was singing out loud, and she had been at my back for a while, then she said, "Cliff, you're singing because you are happy to be leaving us?" I said Oh no, it's because it's the last Friday of the month, which is our family's monthly fasting and thanksgiving prayer day, and I'm just worshiping God. Then she said, "You should ask your God to help you get credit today." I was told that Carthy was an atheist, but she was actually an agnostic, bordering atheism as I later discovered. She was referring to the target given to employees to get customers to apply for the store credit card. The US economy wasn't doing well in 2008, the country was heading into a recession, and Americans were wary of credit cards. It wasn't easy to get one credit card application in a month. In fact, I do not know of any employee who succeeded with one credit application in the past month. The company was struggling financially at that time and was looking to downsize. And employees would be retained based on how well they met the target. I smiled and was not bothered by what she said; it was my last day. However, after reading my Bible during my lunch break as usual. I went to use the restroom, and I suddenly remembered what she had said. I believe it was the Holy Spirit who reminded me of her statement. I never thought about what she said, nor had I made any effort to get credit applications. Then, I realized that she must have said this to prove to me that there is no God.

And I looked up to heaven and prayed, God, you know that I have no need of getting credit, but if you want to prove to Carthy that you exist, help me to get credit without me asking anyone to apply for it. I went back to work and never asked anyone to apply for credit. Then, at 5:45 pm, which was 15 minutes before the end of my shift. The two associates who were to take over from me were already there waiting to start their shift at 6 pm. And while we were there, Carthy came down to the register and asked, "Cliff, did you get any credit today?" And I said no, and she said, "If you don't get any credit before you leave today, I will conclude that there is no God." The two associates waiting to take over from me were shocked beyond words, and their mouths dropped open. They wondered what was going on and knew that it was almost impossible for me to get one within

15 minutes. Then I prayed, God, if You want to prove to Carthy that You exist, send someone to apply for credit without me asking. Just as I was finishing my prayer, a customer walked in and from the door, asked, "If I apply for credit today, how much discount will you give me?" My coworkers were perplexed. Then I said to the customer, Come on in, you will get a 15% discount.

She gladly came, and we started the credit application process. Credit card applications, on average, last for about 2 minutes, and customers could barely wait. However, the devil showed up in this application to discourage the customer, and we encountered issues. However, instead of being discouraged, she encouraged me not to worry and said she was not in a hurry. Then she went and sat down on the sofa at the back, and said that I should let her know when I am done. The Almighty God was in full control of the situation. It took about 30 minutes to get her approved, and she made her payment and left. It was now around 6:20 pm. Then I paged Carthy, our supervisor, to come to the register. She believed that I had left at 6 pm without getting any credit and thought it was the other associates who had paged her. She was surprised to see me when she came down, and I raised up the credit documents, and asked her, "Do you now believe there is God?" She burst into tears and started crying publicly. I took her to a private corner, comforted her, and preached the gospel to her. She shared her story and life challenges with me. I explained to her that God did it because of her. He answered my prayer and granted me the credit application success because He cared about her. Then I prayed for her and left.

When I got to my car at the parking lot, I realized that I had forgotten the clothes I bought from the store in the staff room, so I went back to pick them up. When the two young female associates who were waiting to take over from me saw me coming. They ran to me with great joy and jumped on me, thanking and showing me the credits they both got. They explained to me that when I left, they both said that they should also pray to God and see if He would help them, and they prayed. In about five minutes, between the time I walked to my car and walked back, one got two credits and the other got three. They knew it was nothing short of a miracle. They witnessed God manifest His power and glory through me and keyed into it. The black girl of the two associates there and then promised me that she will not abort the baby. She got pregnant for her boyfriend, and I earlier overheard her discussing plans to abort the baby. She had earlier refused the counsel to not kill the baby. But after seeing the power and glory of God, she surrendered to Him in obedience. The gospel of our Lord and Savior Jesus Christ cannot be silenced. Therein is the power to save life even unto everlasting life.

I also had a similar experience when I worked with the State of Massachusetts. We were prohibited from having religious discussions or preaching the gospel. Employees were not even allowed to wear a T-shirt or a cap that had Jesus printed on it. Of course, I respectfully discussed my faith and preached the gospel of Jesus to everyone possible for the five years I worked there. Acts 5:29, *"Then Peter and the other apostles answered and said, We ought to obey God rather than men."*

Matthew 28:19-20

[19]Go ye therefore, and teach all nations, baptizing them in the name of the Father, and of the Son, and of the Holy Ghost: [20]Teaching them to observe all things whatsoever I

have commanded you: and, lo, I am with you alway, even unto the end of the world. Amen."

The gospel of our Lord and Savior Jesus Christ cannot be silenced. I prayed every day, asking God to create an opportunity for me to preach the gospel at work. God being gracious, would always stir my coworkers and supervisor to seek personal counsel from me. Counsel of which the answers can only be found in Christ. Their questions always create the entry point for the gospel. On one occasion, I worked with one of the supervisors, and God created an entry point for the gospel through his question. I answered his question through the lens of the gospel, and he kept asking me more questions because he wanted to know more. He would often look around to see if anyone was coming, and would say, "I can't believe that I am the one sitting here and discussing religion with you." Then, he would ask another question, and I would answer. This went on until the close of our shift, and when his fellow supervisors came to hang out with him as usual. He said to them that he thinks the person he should be hanging out with now is me.

The State of Massachusetts, where I worked, wants nothing to do with Jesus; in fact, they hate Jesus. But they love Christmas! Every Christmas season, they will decorate the workplace with Christmas trees, themes, and imagery. They exchange Christmas wishes and gifts. They organize Christmas celebration events, play Christmas songs, give food, drinks, and gifts. However, they want nothing to do with Jesus, His gospel, and His commandments. And yet, some Christians say that Jesus is the reason for the season. These are empirical evidences that many people can relate to. I am not talking about abstract situations or theories. These are things most people have observed, experienced, and can equally relate to. It is the same across government, public, and private business organizations. Surely, the empirical evidence of the secular organizations' love for Christmas does not point to Jesus as the reason for the season. Then, the question is, who is the reason for the season?

CHAPTER 5

THE CHRISTMAS SONGS EVIDENCE

T
he Christmas songs provide ample empirical evidence for what the reason for the season is not. The empirical evidence of the Christmas songs is more than adequate to prove that Jesus is not the reason for the season. Yes, the Christmas songs you know and hear every year. What messages do most of the Christmas songs convey to the world about Jesus? Amazingly, most of the Christmas songs we've listened to and sang have nothing whatsoever to do with Jesus Christ. Most of the people who sing and produce them hate Jesus and want nothing to do with Him. However, they love Christmas and enjoy composing Christmas songs. Most people who love to play and listen to Christmas songs hate Jesus and have nothing to do with Him and His law, but they love Christmas. Then, what messages do these Christmas songs convey, and why does the secular world love them? Let's examine a few of the most played Christmas songs we have heard and sang to see if they project Jesus as the reason for the season.

5.1: The Jingle Bells Christmas Song

Oh! Jingle bells, jingle bells　　　　*Dashing through the snow*

Jingle all the way　　　　　　　　*In a one-horse open sleigh*

Oh, what fun it is to ride　　　　　*O'er the fields we go*

In a one-horse open sleigh, hey　　*Laughing all the way*

Jingle bells, jingle bells　　　　　*Bells on bobtails ring*

Jingle all the way　　　　　　　　*Making spirits bright*

Oh, what fun it is to ride　　　　　*What fun it is to ride and sing*

In a one-horse open sleigh　　　　　*A sleighing song tonight*

The "Jingle Bells" Christmas song is one of the most commonly played Christmas songs worldwide. Now, what has jingle bell, jingle bell, got to do with Jesus? What is the meaning of the lyrics, and what message is it proclaiming about Jesus? What does this song have to do with Jesus Christ? Could someone who has never heard the song and doesn't know it's a Christmas song ever hear its lyrics and associate it with Jesus? Could someone learn anything about Jesus from this song? Can this song make anyone contemplate what Jesus did for humanity? In what way does this song glorify Jesus and fill the world with knowledge of Him? Jesus was not once mentioned in the song, and it did not remotely allude to the Christian faith. However, it's a Christmas song to celebrate the birth of Jesus Christ. And some Christians say, Jesus is the reason for the Christmas season celebration?

The Jingle Bells song definitely has a message, but it's not about Jesus. The song is all about playing in the snow, laughing all the way, and taking the girls out, with bells on bobtail's ringing, and making spirits happy. The song is embedded with sexual innuendo, "laughing all the way, and taking the girls out," which is projected to corrupt innocent little boys into developing an interest in girls. Otherwise, it would have said "taking the children out," and why not "taking the boys out," if it's not to corrupt innocent boys. Now tell me, what has taking the girls out got to do with Jesus? What gospel message does it bring about Christianity, or the birth of Jesus Christ? Many readers of this book can empirically verify the effect of this sexual innuendo. They have used the Christmas celebration as an opportunity to take their girlfriends out and have committed sexual immorality in romance and fornication. Songs like Jingle Bells had earlier conditioned them to see Christmas as a period to have fun with their lover. They see nothing sacred about the season, and truthfully, it is so. Superficially, the Christmas season celebration may seem to be about Jesus, but at its core, it has nothing to do with Him. The question is, which spirits are they making happy? Of course, this song can never make the Spirit of God in Christians happy. Therefore, which spirits are they making happy? There is no light of God's Word in the song. That is why the secular world that hates Jesus and has nothing to do with Him loves it. The song does not testify of Jesus because Christmas is of darkness, and there is no light in those who compose the songs.

Isaiah 8:20

To the law and to the testimony: if they speak not according to this word, it is because there is no light in them.

5.2: Rudolph The Red-Nosed Reindeer Christmas Songs

You know Dasher and Dancer
And Prancer and Vixen
Comet and Cupid
Donner and Blitzen
But do you recall
The most famous reindeer of all?

Rudolph, the red-nosed reindeer
Had a very shiny nose
And if you ever saw it
You would even say it glows
All of the other reindeer

Used to laugh and call him names
They never let poor Rudolph
Join in any reindeer games

Then one foggy Christmas Eve
Santa came to say
"Rudolph with your nose so bright
Won't you guide my sleigh tonight?"
Then how the reindeer loved him
As they shouted out with glee
"Rudolph, the red-nosed reindeer
You'll go down in history!"

Rudolph the Red-Nosed Reindeer is one of the most played Christmas songs. It was one of the Christmas songs that was often played at the store where I worked in my early days in the US. Jingle Bells and Rudolph the Red-Nosed Reindeer were their favorites. Now what has Rudolph the Red-Nosed Reindeer got to do with Jesus? Tell me, what has Rudolph the Red-Nosed Reindeer got to do with Jesus Christ? Nothing, obviously; nonetheless, it has a lot to do with Christmas and the reason for the season. The real reason for the season will be revealed further down the road as part of the empirical evidence. Whatever the secular world loves should always be a trigger for a heavenly-minded Christian to pause, think, research, and pray before getting involved.

The song starts with, You know, Dasher and Dancer, and Prancer and Vixen, Comet and Cupid, Donner and Blitzen. Now, what has any of these names got to do with Jesus or the gospel? All these are names of idols, which the pagans worship, and what have idols got to do with Jesus? Take, for instance, Cupid, an ancient Roman god of love, commonly represented by a winged, naked infant boy with a bow and arrow. This winged naked infant boy with a bow and arrow is often used to depict the god of love during the Valentine's Day season celebrations. That is Cupid, no wonder the secular world loves Christmas. And what has Cupid, the Roman idol of love, got to do with Jesus? And yet, some Christians have not paused to think? They even play Rudolph the Red-Nosed Reindeer in their homes and cars as they celebrate and enjoy Christmas with their families. Shouldn't this Christmas song alone have caused heavenly-minded Christians to stop and think before getting involved? The song then introduces Santa as the great one who came to lift Rudolph the Red-Nosed Reindeer from his misery. Who then is Santa, and what does he have to do with Jesus Christ? Although a red-nosed reindeer has nothing to do with Jesus Christ or the gospel. Nonetheless, the so-called Christmas song did not even have Jesus Christ as the Mighty One who rescued Rudolph the Red-Nosed Reindeer from his misery. It was Santa! And who is he? And what do all these idols and Santa have to do with Jesus Christ and Christianity?

2 Corinthians 6:14-16

[14]Be ye not unequally yoked together with unbelievers: for what fellowship hath righteousness with unrighteousness? and what communion hath light with darkness? [15]And what concord hath Christ with Belial? or what part hath he that believeth with an infidel? [16]And what agreement hath the temple of God with idols? for ye are the temple of the living

God; as God hath said, I will dwell in them, and walk in them; and I will be their God, and they shall be my people.

5.3: The Twelve Days Of Christmas Song

On the first day of Christmas, my true love gave to me: A partridge in a pear tree

On the second day of Christmas, my true love gave to me: Two turtle doves, ...

On the third day of Christmas, my true love gave to me: Three French hens, ...

On the fourth day of Christmas, my true love gave to me: Four calling birds, ...

On the fifth day of Christmas, my true love gave to me: Five gold rings, ...

On the sixth day of Christmas, my true love gave to me: Six geese a laying, ...

On the seventh day of Christmas, my true love gave to me: Seven swans a-swimming, ...

On the eighth day of Christmas, my true love gave to me: Eight maids a-milking, ...

On the ninth day of Christmas (mee, mee, mee, mee, mee): Nine ladies dancing, ...

On the tenth day of Christmas, my true love gave to me: Ten lords a-leaping, ...

On the eleventh day of Christmas, my true love gave to me: Eleven pipers piping, ...

On the twelfth day of Christmas, my true love gave to me: Twelve drummers drumming, ...

Now, what has twelve days got to do with Jesus' birth? How come the twelve days of Christmas? Could twelve days be remotely associated with the biblical accounts of the birth of Jesus? Did Mary and Joseph travel for twelve days before they got to the manger where Jesus was born? Or was Mary in hard labor for twelve days before she gave birth to Jesus? According to the song, their true love on the first day of Christmas gave them a partridge in a pear tree. On the second day, two turtle doves; the third, three French hens; the fourth, four calling birds; the fifth, five gold rings; the sixth, six geese a laying; and the rest of the nonsense till the twelfth day. What do the twelve days signify, and where do you find this in the Bible? These songs, which have nothing to do with Jesus and Christianity, fill the airwaves during the Christmas season in celebration of the birth of Jesus. Should this not cause a heavenly-minded Christian to pause, think, and ask, Is Jesus really the reason for the season?

The secular world, like Hollywood, loves Christmas songs and movies. They compose the Christmas songs, and yet they hate Jesus, and you say Jesus is the reason for the season? The celebrities of this world who dress naked, who are polluting the world with immorality, and have nothing to do with Jesus. Yet they love Christmas and Christmas songs. Hollywood is all about drugs, money, sex, fame, and everything vain. Everything they promote is vanity and against the way of God. Even their Christmas songs, albums, shows, plays, and movies are actually a mockery of Christianity. They are all about self and money; they dress almost nude as they pose, in their Christmas dresses and decorations. Then they sing your Christmas songs to glorify who? Jesus or Satan? In their Jezebelic dressing and appearance, they sing songs that hardly mention the name Jesus. And you say they are celebrating the birthday of Jesus, while promoting sin and normalizing evil? The people who hate Jesus so badly, who walk against him, against His truth, against what he teaches, are the ones singing your Christmas songs for you. And yet you say Jesus is the reason for the season? You have been deceived!

Christmas!

Whatever the secular world loves should alarm a heaven-minded Christian to pause and think. Then, research and pray to God for understanding before getting involved. The Bible is the Ultimate Source of Authority for reference to truth and must inform every action of heavenly-minded Christians. My emphasis had been on heavenly-minded Christians because not all so-called Christian desires heaven. The empirical evidence for most popular Christmas songs we have examined in this chapter reveals the Christlessness in the December 25th Christmas season celebration. The Christmas songs' empirical evidence obviously proves that Jesus Christ is not the reason for the season. Then, who is the reason for the Christmas season celebration?

CHAPTER 6

THE CHRISTMAS IMAGES EVIDENCE

The images, that is, the objects and artifacts used for decorations for the Christmas season's celebration, are empirical evidence for the Christlessness of Christmas. Objects like sox, artifacts of the sun, stars, and moon, and graven images of Mary, Joseph, and baby Jesus, to mention a few. These and others represent the imagery of the Christmas season celebration. They characterize the December 25th Christmas season celebration as homes and offices are lit up and decorated with these images. What do these sox and artifacts promote, and is there a biblical reference for them? What is the purpose of the sox, and what do those Christmas images have to do with Jesus Christ?

6.1: The Graven Images

The Christmas season is always filled with colorful artifacts and images of biblical characters. Graven images of Mary, Joseph, and baby Jesus, the Wise Men, and angels, often fill many homes and churches during the Christmas season. The Bible clearly states that we should not make any graven image of things in heaven, on earth, or the like of it, and we should not bow down or worship it. This is the second commandment of the Ten given to man by God. In transgression against this commandment, people make graven images of Mary, Joseph, and baby Jesus. And some people also bow down and worship it during their Christmas celebration.

Exodus 20:1-6

¹And God spake all these words, saying, ²I am the LORD thy God, which have brought thee out of the land of Egypt, out of the house of bondage. ³Thou shalt have no other gods before me. ⁴Thou shalt not make unto thee any graven image, or any likeness of any thing that is in heaven above, or that is in the earth beneath, or that is in the water under the earth: ⁵Thou shalt not bow down thyself to them, nor serve them: for I the LORD thy God am a jealous God, visiting the iniquity of the fathers upon the children unto the third and fourth generation of them that hate me;

During Christmas, people decorate their homes with images of Mary, Joseph, and baby Jesus, the Wise Men with gifts, and angels in their midst. Some bow down and worship this setup. Not only have they broken God's command by making these images, but they also bow to them and worship them. This is idolatry! And what has idolatry got to do with Jesus Christ and Christianity? Can we transgress God's commandment to honor and celebrate Jesus? Is there a biblical precedent to reference such a practice? Obviously, none. There is no biblical reference for such an idolatrous celebration of the birth of Jesus. Neither the Apostles nor the New Testament church practiced this at any point in their time. From where, then, did this practice emanate to infiltrate Christendom? Can you not see the handwriting of Satan everywhere? And yet you say, Jesus is the reason for the season. The graven images and their worship during the Christmas celebration are empirical evidence that Jesus is not the reason for the season. Many have observed and experienced this idolatrous practice in churches and homes during the December 25th Christmas celebration. This practice is not a historical account nor a narrative. Rather, that which we've all observed and experienced. Churches and homes are literally turned into temples of idols during the Christmas season. And what has Christ got to do with idols and their worshipers?

2 Corinthians 6:14-16

14Be ye not unequally yoked together with unbelievers: for what fellowship hath righteousness with unrighteousness? and what communion hath light with darkness? 15And what concord hath Christ with Belial? or what part hath he that believeth with an infidel? 16And what agreement hath the temple of God with idols? for ye are the temple of the living God; as God hath said, I will dwell in them, and walk in them; and I will be their God, and they shall be my people.

6.2: The Love Of Mammon And Pride

The secular world loves the Christmas season more so because of merchandising; it is a money-generating business. The Christmas season is a boom season for business. Business organizations, along with many businessmen and women, are in it for the money. The Christmas season celebration and merchandising generate billions to trillions in revenue in any world currency. The Christmas season celebration is an idolatrous worship, and the god they worship is that of mammon. It is impossible to worship God and mammon. Therefore, it's not Jesus that is being worshiped and honored in the December

Christmas!

25th Christmas season celebration. Jesus! is not the reason for the season.

Matthew 6:24

No man can serve two masters: for either he will hate the one, and love the other; or else he will hold to the one, and despise the other. Ye cannot serve God and mammon.

The spirit of mammon is active during the Christmas season, inspiring innovative designs to satisfy the greed of business owners and the lust and pride of the people. Some people will spend beyond their financial ability and go into debt just to satisfy their lust and pride to buy things for themselves and others. This same spirit motivates individuals to lavish spending on decorating their homes with Christmas artifacts. The same could be said for communities, towns, cities, and organizations. They strive to satisfy their pride, competing to outdo their neighbor in Christmas decorations. Sometimes there are open contests to determine the "best decorated" home and city for Christmas. And sometimes it's just subtle; everyone is silently competing to outdo their neighbor. Some cities and towns become major tourist attractions during the Christmas season. People would travel from far and near to view the colorful, artistic Christmas decorations in those locations. In what way does this bring glory to Jesus Christ and promote His course for holiness? Certainly, the Christmas season celebration is not because of Jesus. It's all about vanity, pride, money, and idolatry. The LORD Jesus made himself of no reputation, humbled himself, and God said we should be of the same humble mind and spirit.

Philippians 2:5-8

⁵Let this mind be in you, which was also in Christ Jesus: ⁶Who, being in the form of God, thought it not robbery to be equal with God: ⁷But made himself of no reputation, and took upon him the form of a servant, and was made in the likeness of men: ⁸And being found in fashion as a man, he humbled himself, and became obedient unto death, even the death of the cross.

Is this the mind of those who spend lavishly on clothes, gift items, and Christmas artifacts and images to decorate their homes and businesses? Are they doing it in the same mind as Christ, who humbled Himself to be born in a manger? Is it done to promote Christ or promote mammon and pride? Is it the Spirit of God at work? And if not the Spirit of God, then whose? Who is being glorified by the Christmas season's prideful, idolatrous competitions? It must be the god of mammon and pride, Satan.

CHAPTER 7

THE SANTA CLAUS EVIDENCE

Santa Claus, a fictitious character also known as Father Christmas, is the most prominent figure and image for the Christmas season celebrations. He has been the central image and person of Christmas. Parents talk to their children about Santa Claus and present gifts to them in the name of Santa Claus. They lie to their children that Santa will visit their home at midnight to reward the good ones with gifts. Christmas events are organized for children, and Santa Claus will be there to give them gifts. The children look forward to meeting Santa, who will reward them with gifts for their good behavior. Posters, flyers, gift wrappers, merchandise, TV, and social media are all flooded with the image of Santa Claus during the Christmas season. Santa Claus plays the role of the mighty one of Christmas, Father Christmas, the rewarder! The questions are, who is Santa Claus, or who does he represent, and what has he got to do with Jesus Christ? The Santa Claus empirical evidence points directly to the real reason for the season.

7.1: Who Is Santa Claus?

There is a lot more to Santa Claus than the Old man in the red and white costume. There is a lot more to Santa, and with far-reaching destructive consequences, than just a fictitious Christmas character used to deceive children. Santa Claus, the legendary figure associated with Saint Nicholas, is the most prominent figure of the Christmas season. Santa Claus, also known as Father Christmas, is the central figure of Christmas. Santa Claus or Father Christmas is the empirical evidence that directly points to the reason for the Christmas season. Santa is an anagram of Satan, and Claus is also an anagram of Lucas, which is a reference to Lucifer. Could it be coincidental that Santa and Claus are both anagrams of the devil's names? Remove the N at the end of Satan and place it after the first A, and you get Santa. Rearrange the Claus, and you get Lucas, which is Lucifer. So, you have Santa Claus, representing the devil's two names, Satan and Lucifer, as the legend of Christmas. And people say Jesus is the reason for the season? What communion has light and darkness, and what agreement has Christ with the devil?

2 Corinthians 6:14-16

[14]Be ye not unequally yoked together with unbelievers: for what fellowship hath righteousness with unrighteousness? and what communion hath light with darkness? [15]And what concord hath Christ with Belial? or what part hath he that believeth with an infidel? [16]And what agreement hath the temple of God with idols? for ye are the temple of the living God; as God hath said, I will dwell in them, and walk in them; and I will be their God, and they shall be my people.

Christmas!

According to sources, in the occult world, anagrams and symbols are usually used to conceal the truth so as to deceive people. I have never been part of the occult/satanic world to validate this empirically; nevertheless, does this not sound plausible? Deception is the most powerful weapon in Satan's arsenal. The Bible implores us to put on the whole armor of God to defend ourselves against the deceptions (wiles) of Satan. Ephesians 6:11, *"Put on the whole armour of God, that ye may be able to stand against the wiles of the devil."* Anagrams are words or phrases formed from rearranging other words or phrases. Anagrams are often used as secret codes or messages to conceal information. In the occult/satanic world, anagrams and symbols are usually used to hide information. They use them to hide truth, meaning, and purpose, to confuse and deceive people. There are many resources that are available on the history of the pagan origin and the deity of Christmas. Hence, I will advise you to research the origin of Christmas for yourself to be more informed. Nonetheless, we will continue to focus on empirical evidence; things we have observed and experienced. Santa, being an anagram of Satan, and Claus, an anagram of Lucas, which is Lucifer, concealed the Devil. Satan is a deceiver and the father of all lies, and very subtle. Would he not be operating in such a disguised manner to deceive?

John 8:44

Ye are of your father the devil, and the lusts of your father ye will do. He was a murderer from the beginning, and abode not in the truth, because there is no truth in him. When he speaketh a lie, he speaketh of his own: for he is a liar, and the father of it.

2 Corinthians 11:14

And no marvel; for Satan himself is transformed into an angel of light.

Satan has transformed himself into Santa, a false angel of light, acting as the good guy, the rewarder of good works. Through this deception, he has turned the hearts of many parents and children away from the living God to himself. Why would Satan not do so? Does he not want the world to worship him? If Satan wasn't afraid to tempt Jesus to get Him to worship him. Would he not attempt to deceive humanity into worshiping him?

Matthew 4:8-10

[8]Again, the devil taketh him up into an exceeding high mountain, and sheweth him all the kingdoms of the world, and the glory of them; [9]And saith unto him, All these things will I give thee, if thou wilt fall down and worship me. [10]Then saith Jesus unto him, Get thee hence, Satan: for it is written, Thou shalt worship the Lord thy God, and him only shalt thou serve.

Satan was unsuccessful in his effort to deceive Jesus into worshiping him. However, he has been very successful in deceiving many Christian families into worshipping him. Satan transformed himself into Santa, the great one of Christmas, the rewarder of good works. And through this, Satan ascribed to himself the attributes of God, and many Christians, knowingly or unknowingly, are worshiping him. Saint Nicholas, the early Christian bishop of Greek descent, also known as Saint Nick, is the historic figure who was said to have been transformed into Santa Claus. Nicholas is abbreviated as Nick, and Old Nick means the Devil. The only possible biblical reference to Nick is in Revelation 2:6,15, where it talks about the doctrine of the Nicolaitans. Maybe that's Nicholas, I don't know, just my thoughts. Look up Old Nick in the dictionary, or Google it. You will see that it means the Devil or Satan, and that the origin of the name is uncertain. Maybe it's just another coincidence that Nicholas is abbreviated as Nick, and Old Nick means the devil. If it's just a coincidence, then it is an excellent one. Is it also a coincidence that Santa flies in the air, and Satan is the prince of the power of the air? Is it also another coincidence that the spirit that works in the children of disobedience is the prince of the power of the air, Satan?

Ephesians 2:2

Wherein in time past ye walked according to the course of this world, according to the prince of the power of the air, the spirit that now worketh in the children of disobedience:

The prince of the power of the air, the spirit that now worked in the children of disobedience. Do you see that? And yet, Santa Claus is the prince of the air. He flies from the North Pole, and he flies in the air on a sleigh driven by elves. Elves represent spirits in the world of witchcraft. And it's just another coincidence that nothing else could power Santa's sleigh but witchcraft spirits. The elves are central to Santa's power. They provide magical abilities, labor, and logistical support for the Christmas season, enabling him to deliver gifts to children worldwide. Is that not what happens during Christmas celebrations? It is about Rudolph the Red-Nosed Reindeer and Santa Claus bringing gifts to your children. The children are deceived into praying to Santa and wishing Santa would bring them gifts overnight. This is the reason why one of the most prominent Christmas songs is "Rudolph the Red-nosed Reindeer." Reindeer is an elf.

Then one foggy Christmas Eve

Santa came to say

"Rudolph with your nose so bright

Won't you guide my sleigh tonight?"

Then how the reindeer loved him

As they shouted out with glee

"Rudolph, the red-nosed reindeer

You'll go down in history!"

You may have observed Santa Claus portrayed in movies, with the magical powers to reward children for being good all year. In witchcraft, "elf" refers to a variety of supernatural beings. A concept also held in ancient European folklore, where elves were seen as causes of illness and wielders of magical powers. In contemporary paganism and witchcraft, elves are approached as spiritual entities with whom one can connect for magical powers, healing, and guidance. Santa flies through the air in a sleigh powered by elves, which are believed to be witchcraft spirits. Satan is the prince of the power of the air, the spirit that works in the children of disobedience. Santa flies in the air and comes into your chimney to reward your children for being good. It's just a coincidence, right? No, Cliff, it's just a coincidence, you're imagining things; Santa is not Satan, it's just an excellent coincidence. These are things you have observed and experienced yourself.

We have seen that Santa is an anagram of Satan, and Claus is an anagram of Lucas, which is Lucifer. Furthermore, we have seen that Saint Nick, the historic figure associated with Santa Claus, can also be associated with Old Nick, meaning Satan, the Devil. Satan's names and attributes are associated with everything about Santa Claus. If it quacks like a duck and walks like a duck, then it is a duck. Let us examine the attributes of Santa Claus and see if we can find the Devil's DNA in them.

7.2: The Attributes Of Santa Claus

Santa Claus has assumed attributes that are unique to God alone. Santa claims to have all the unique attributes that made God who He is. Attributes that made God differ from all celestial and terrestrial beings. The assumption of these attributes by Santa exposes the DNA of Satan, Lucifer, in Santa Claus. According to the Bible, the only being that had ever desired and attempted to be like God is Lucifer, the Devil. Satan wanted to take the place of God, and for this very reason, he was cast out from heaven to the earth

Isaiah 14:12-14

[12]How art thou fallen from heaven, O Lucifer, son of the morning! how art thou cut down to the ground, which didst weaken the nations! [13]For thou hast said in thine heart, I will ascend into heaven, I will exalt my throne above the stars of God: I will sit also upon the mount of the congregation, in the sides of the north: [14]I will ascend above the heights of the clouds; I will be like the Most High.

We can perfectly fit Santa Claus in this Bible text. Lucifer said in his heart that he will ascend into heaven and exalt his throne above the stars of God; he will also sit above God's congregation in the sides of the north. That is, from every corner of the world, he will be on top in the north. And he will take the place of God, be like the Most High. Ezekiel 14:13-14, *"¹³For thou hast said in thine heart, I will ascend into heaven, I will exalt my throne above the stars of God: I will sit also upon the mount of the congregation, in the sides of the north: ¹⁴I will ascend above the heights of the clouds; I will be like the Most High."* The stars of God are the righteous children of God, Christians. Daniel 12:3, *"And they that be wise shall shine as the brightness of the firmament; and they that turn many to righteousness as the stars for ever and ever."* Lucifer had said that he will exalt himself above the children of God and sit above the congregation, that is, the Church of Christ, on every side of the north. Is it a coincidence that Santa Claus exalted himself above the Church, flies to every home in the world from all sides of the North Pole, exalted himself as the Most High, and is being worshipped? 2 Corinthians 11:14, *"And no marvel; for Satan himself is transformed into an angel of light."* Lucifer is transformed into a false angel of light, Santa, to achieve his goal of reigning over the Church of Christ and being worshipped like God. Santa Claus is Lucifer, Satan the Devil! Santa Claus, that is Satan, is the reason for the December 25th Christmas celebration. He is the central figure and image of Christmas, the great one of Christmas, and the rewarder of those who are good.

The congregations, that is, the children of God, are busy spending the Christmas season worshipping Santa Claus, Lucifer. They teach their children about Santa Claus and pray to him for all their desires, wishes, and needs. This is exactly what Satan desires; he wants to be exalted and worshipped in place of God Almighty. Lucifer said he will exalt himself above the stars of God (children of God) and the congregation (church), so they will look up to him, teach their children about him, pray to him, and worship him. Lucifer, through lies and deception, has transformed into Santa Claus to achieve his desire through the December 25th Christmas season celebration. Here is the outline of Santa's God-like attributes, which clearly reveal the DNA of Lucifer.

1. Santa Is Eternal:

Santa's beginning is unknown; no one knows how he came to be. He does not get older than he already is and does not die. He lives from generation to generation. He is the same every year. Santa Claus is not God; how then is he without a beginning and without an end? Oh!! Satan! he wants to be like the Most High.

2. Santa Is Omniscient:

Santa is all-knowing. He knows all the children in the world who have been good and those who have been bad. Ah! Is this not the very definition of omniscient? This attribute makes Santa like God. In fact, he is meant to replace God, and indeed Santa Claus has taken the place of God in many Christian families. The children look forward to the omniscient Santa as their rewarder at the end of the year.

3. Santa Is Omnipresent:

Santa is in every home in the world on December 25th, delivering gifts to all the good children. He is everywhere at the same time, just like God. Santa Claus has replaced God in many homes; he has bestowed on himself the character of God. Who else aspires to replace God? Oh!! it's Satan again. Maybe Santa is Satan's double.

4. Santa Answers Prayers:

Prayers are offered to Santa. Parents ask their children to ask Santa for what they wish for Christmas. Is that not prayers? Parents deceive their children into believing that Satan answers their prayers. Then, they go to buy the gifts their children had wished/prayed for, and deceive their children that it is a gift from Santa Claus. A child prays to Santa for a gift, maybe a new iPad. The parents will go to the store, or online, buy an iPad, and hide it until the morning of December 25th. In the morning, when the child unwraps their gifts, they rejoice and thank Santa for answering their prayers. Santa has gifted them for being good, all thanks to the prayer-answering Santa Claus! The Bible says that all flesh must pray to God. Psalm 65:1-2, *"Praise waiteth for thee, O God, in Sion: and unto thee shall the vow be performed. ²O thou that hearest prayer, unto thee shall all flesh come."* Unfortunately, many parents have deceitfully taken their children to Santa instead of God. The praise that awaits God, who hears and answers prayers, they have given to Santa Claus, who has usurped the place of God.

What is to be said of these parents who lie and deceive their children? Is lying and deception not a sin? Have they not become the children of the Devil and doing the work of their father? Parents who sin continually by lying and deceiving their children about the fictitious Santa will be judged for their sins if they do not repent.

John 8:44

Ye are of your father the devil, and the lusts of your father ye will do. He was a murderer from the beginning, and abode not in the truth, because there is no truth in him.

When he speaketh a lie, he speaketh of his own: for he is a liar, and the father of it.

Revelation 21:8

But the fearful, and unbelieving, and the abominable, and murderers, and whoremongers, and sorcerers, and idolaters, and all liars, shall have their part in the lake which burneth with fire and brimstone: which is the second death.

Revelation 21:8 says that "All Liars," which includes parents who lie to their children about Santa Claus, shall have their part in the Lake of Fire. Truly, there is a lot more to Santa than an old man in a red and white costume. Lucifer had transformed himself into Santa Claus to deceive many into worshipping him as God. And have succeeded in damning many souls in hell through this deception. The following scriptures are observed and experienced through the characteristics of Santa Claus. Ezekiel 14:13-14, *"¹³For thou hast said in thine heart, I will ascend into heaven, I will exalt my throne above the stars of God: I will sit also upon the mount of the congregation, in the sides of the north: ¹⁴I will ascend above the heights of the clouds; I will be like the Most High."* 2 Corinthians 11:14, *"And no marvel; for Satan himself is transformed into an angel of light."*

You just read the attributes of Santa, which usurped God's attributes in all ways, taking the place of God, being like God, and acting like God. Is that not what Satan said he would do, to exalt himself above the clouds and be like the Most High? Are all these just mere coincidences? Most definitely not! The Santa Claus empirical evidence clearly reveals that Jesus is not the real reason for the December 25th Christmas season celebrations. The real reason is to exalt Lucifer as the Most High God and to honor and worship him. Let us now examine the End-Time Christmas celebration evidence to validate these findings from the Santa Claus empirical evidence.

CHAPTER 8

THE END-TIME CHRISTMAS
CELEBRATION EVIDENCE

One remarkable thing about the End-Time is that evil is celebrated openly. In times past, evil was done in secrecy and concealed from the public's eyes. Satan hid himself from being noticed and deceived people into believing that he did not exist. But now in this End-Time, Satan is no longer in hiding; he is being worshiped and celebrated openly. Satanism (witchcraft, etc.), which used to be a secret cult, is now openly publicized. Good and light are now being portrayed as evil by the media, government, organizations, and individuals. And evil and darkness are now being projected as good by the world. Jesus and Christianity are projected as evil, while Satan and all manner of evil (sexual immorality/perversion, LGBTQ, transgenderism, atheism, idolatry, etc.) are projected as good. God's message to those who call good and light evil, and call evil and darkness good, couldn't be clearer than this:

Isaiah 5:20-24

²⁰Woe unto them that call evil good, and good evil; that put darkness for light, and light for darkness; that put bitter for sweet, and sweet for bitter! ²¹Woe unto them that are wise in their own eyes, and prudent in their own sight! ²²Woe unto them that are mighty to drink wine, and men of strength to mingle strong drink: ²³Which justify the wicked for reward, and take away the righteousness of the righteous from him! ²⁴Therefore as the fire devoureth the stubble, and the flame consumeth the chaff, so their root shall be as rottenness, and their blossom shall go up as dust: because they have cast away the law of the LORD of hosts, and despised the word of the Holy One of Israel.

All these are happening in this End-Time because Satan, through his wiles, has secretly captured the majority of the world to himself, including those who proclaim to be Christians. And since his time to publicly reign over the world in the End-Time is at hand. He is now unveiling himself to the world because he knows that many approve of him. This trend can also be observed in the End-Time December 25ᵗʰ Christmas season celebrations. Satan has begun to introduce himself publicly as the real reason for the season, a thing which was once hidden in the shadows in times past.

8.1: The Unveiling Of Baby Satan For Christmas

During the December 2021 Christmas season celebrations in the United States. The Satanic Temple installed a baby Baphomet next to baby Jesus in the Illinois State Capitol. The truth of who the December 25th Christmas celebration is all about is now being unveiled. The news was on Fox; you can find it on the Fox News Channel. The Fox News anchor said it's a mockery of religious expression and blasphemous. He said it's blasphemy because he believed that the Christmas celebrations were about Jesus Christ. Christmas was never about Jesus, as was clearly revealed through the biblical and empirical evidence we have treated so far. Certainly, it was demonic and blasphemous against God to use His name in place of the worship of Satan. However, it wasn't demonic and blasphemous because baby Satan was introduced into the December 25th Christmas celebrations. Christmas has always been demonic and blasphemous from its very beginning; it has always been about the worship of Satan in the name of Christ. The only difference now is that Satan is beginning to emerge out of the shadows as the real reason for the season. Baphomet is the occultic anthropomorphic image of Satan with the head and legs of a goat. It was the baby of it that was unveiled and placed in the Illinois State Capitol, as the one whose birth has been celebrated on December 25th for many centuries.

Baphomet: (Occultic anthropomorphic image of Satan with the head and legs of a goat)

The Baby Baphomet, which was placed in the Illinois State Capitol for the 2021 Christmas Celebrations.

The Satanic Temple was just unveiling the real person who has been celebrated on December 25th. Satan, who has been worshiped and celebrated in the shadows during the December 25th season celebrations, is beginning to emerge and take his place and glory. The baby Devil was unveiled to show you who you've been celebrating. Yes, you can see it yourself. This should shock and revive the many Christians who are being destroyed for lack of knowledge. Hosea 4:6, *"My people are destroyed for lack of knowledge: because thou hast rejected knowledge, I will also reject thee, that thou shalt be no priest to me: seeing thou hast forgotten the law of thy God, I will also forget thy children."* Satan has been silent for many centuries playing his non-existent game, but in this End-Time era. Satan is beginning to project himself publicly as the good fella, as the deliverer, the rewarder, the mighty one of Christmas. That is why he is no longer celebrated in the shadows through Christmas but openly. Satanism is no longer a secret cult in our society. Satan is now projected as good, and people are worshipping and celebrating him openly at Christmas. Morality is now turned upside down; good is called evil, and evil is called good. Therefore, it's the perfect time for the god who is being worshiped and celebrated during the December 25th Christmas season to emerge and take his rightful place. Biblically, and empirically, you cannot find any justifiable evidence that points to Jesus Christ as the reason for the December 25th Christmas season celebrations.

8.2: Disney's Christmas Love For Satan

Disney did a Christmas movie in 2022, which is the year following the unveiling and introduction of the baby Baphomet for Christmas celebrations. In this Disney Christmas movie, some children had placards with different letters written on them. The Children were doing a presentation to Santa Claus and some other people, who were standing before them. And with those placards, they formed the words "WE LOVE YOU SATAN." Then, Santa and the people with him laughed, and Santa said, "spelling!" Then, the children looked at the word they had formed, "SATAN," and they screamed. Then the child holding the N at the end came and stood after the child with the first A, and it became "SANTA." Then, Santa Claus said, "There you go, that's my name."

Disney is showing you who they work for. Protect your children at all costs; they're after your children. It was a perfect act to show you that "SANTA" is just an anagram of "SATAN." Disney just showed the world who they love and celebrate during the December 25th Christmas season celebrations. They said, "WE LOVE YOU SATAN." And you still think Jesus is the reason for the season? They have shown you who they love and celebrate at Christmas. The previous year, the Satanic Temple unveiled and introduced baby Satan, "Baphomet," as the god they worship and celebrate during Christmas. Believe them, believe what you have observed and experienced; Christmas is for the worship and celebration of Satan. Satan has been in the shadows for many centuries, deceiving people that he is nonexistent. However, in this End-Time era, Satan is beginning to project himself publicly. He is now being projected as the good fella, the deliverer, the rewarder, the mighty one of Christmas. Satanism is no longer a secret cult in this End-Time. Satan is now projected as good, and people are worshipping and celebrating him openly, including Christians, through the Christmas celebrations. Biblical evidence had made it clear that the birth of Jesus was not to be celebrated. There is no single Bible reference for the commemorations and celebration of Jesus' birthday. The Satanic Temple and Disney have shown you that it is Satan they love, worship, and celebrate during Christmas. No wonder the world loves Christmas! Whatever the world loves should always alarm a heavenly-minded Christian to pause, research, and pray before getting involved.

James 4:4

Ye adulterers and adulteresses, know ye not that the friendship of the world is enmity with God? whosoever therefore will be a friend of the world is the enemy of God.

2 Corinthians 6:14-16

[14]Be ye not unequally yoked together with unbelievers: for what fellowship hath righteousness with unrighteousness? and what communion hath light with darkness? [15]And what concord hath Christ with Belial? or what part hath he that believeth with an infidel? [16]And what agreement hath the temple of God with idols? for ye are the temple of the living God; as God hath said, I will dwell in them, and walk in them; and I will be their God, and they shall be my people.

CHAPTER 9

THE CHRISTMAS TREE EVIDENCE

The secular world, and many Christians, use Christmas trees in their December 25th Christmas celebrations. The Fir, pine, and spruce trees are popular choices for individuals, churches, organizations, and businesses. They cut green trees, or buy a trimmed and ready one, or a synthetic replica. Then they decorate it with lights, gold, and silver ornaments. They beautify the tree as much as possible, then place gifts under the tree for their children and loved ones. What does this green tree ritual have to do with Jesus Christ of Nazareth? Was Jesus born under a green tree? The so-called Christians and pastors approve of and practice this ritual in their churches and homes. They do this in the name of the Christmas celebrations, and they say it is all about Jesus Christ. Is there a biblical reference for such green tree rituals? Of course there is. And is it for the worship and honor of God?

9.1: The Green Tree Rituals

Green trees are used for heathenistic worship rituals all over the world. People from Africa can easily relate to this. The Wiccans in America use green trees for various rituals and sacrifices. These rituals are secretly done at midnight, the same way Satan has gotten many into doing it at midnight preceding December 25th. People deck their green trees with lights, gold, and silver. Then, at midnight, they secretly go to make sacrifices under it, which is the gifts they drop there. Let's examine what the Bible has to say about the green tree ritual.

Jeremiah 10:1-4

[1]Hear ye the word which the LORD speaketh unto you, O house of Israel: [2]Thus saith the LORD, Learn not the way of the heathen, and be not dismayed at the signs of heaven; for the heathen are dismayed at them. [3]For the customs of the people are vain: for one cutteth a tree out of the forest, the work of the hands of the workman, with the axe. [4]They deck it with silver and with gold; they fasten it with nails and with hammers, that it move not.

God commanded the Israelites not to learn the ways of the heathen. The Israelites were God's people, and now Christians, "those who believe in Jesus," are God's people. God, through the Prophet Jeremiah, spoke to His people not to learn the way of the heathen. What are the ways of the heathen that God is concerned about? Their idolatrous customs, of cutting a tree, decking it with silver and gold, and fastening it to a place where it won't move. According to God, being fascinated by the signs of heaven, cutting trees and decking them with silver and gold, is the vain custom of the heathen. Those who practice such things are heathens, that is, those who do not know God. Many heathenistic customs in Africa and around the world practice these green tree rituals. They not only cut down trees for it, but also go under the green trees at midnight to perform these ritualistic sacrifices. The heathens surrounding the Israelites also practiced going under the green trees to make sacrifices. God warned the Israelites not to learn these heathenistic ways and vain customs. Nonetheless, they learned and practiced them when they had backslidden from following God.

Jeremiah 3:6

The Lord said also unto me in the days of Josiah the king, Hast thou seen that which backsliding Israel hath done? she is gone up upon every high mountain and under every green tree, and there hath played the harlot.

2 Kings 16:3-4

³But he walked in the way of the kings of Israel, yea, and made his son to pass through the fire, according to the abominations of the heathen, whom the LORD cast out from before the children of Israel. ⁴And he sacrificed and burnt incense in the high places, and on the hills, and under every green tree.

This heathen custom is what people have adopted in their December 25th Christmas celebration. Many people have observed these heathenistic practices of going under green trees at midnight to make sacrifices, that is, to offer gifts to the idols they worship. It is this heathen ritualistic sacrifice that subtle Satan has deceitfully brought into Christianity. He deceived Christians into learning and practicing the ways and customs of the heathen. Therefore, many Christians are now fascinated by the signs of heaven, such as the moon, sun, and stars. They cut down a green tree, or buy one, or a synthetic replica; they deck it with silver and gold signs of heaven (moon, sun, and stars as lights). Then, at midnight preceding December 25th, they will secretly go and make sacrifices under it to the idol they worship, Santa, which is Satan.

This heathen practice is what people have adopted in their December 25th Christmas celebration. Whatever the world loves should always cause a heavenly-minded Christian to pause, think, research, and pray. It should be a trigger to ask, What is the spiritual implication? God is telling Christians not to learn the ways of the heathen. Do not learn the ways of the worldly people who do not regard God. Do not be fascinated by the things that fascinate them. They are fascinated by the stars, the moon, the firmament, and the signs of heaven. That is the same thing that fascinates those who cut or buy green trees, and decorate them with the sun, moon, and shiny lights that represent stars. These are the practices of the heathen, i.e., idol worshipers. Is that not what many Christians have adopted for the December 25th Christmas celebrations? And yet they say Jesus is the reason for the season. God is saying that Christians should not be fascinated by the things the heathen, the ungodly secular world, are fascinated by. And they should not practice them. That is exactly what God says in the Bible.

9.2: The Lying Christian Heathens

The lying Christian heathens are those who claim to be Christians and yet join the heathens every year to perform the green tree heathenistic sacrifice rituals. Then lie to their children that their god, Santa Claus, that is, Satan, has rewarded them with gifts for being good. That is what these so-called Christians do: they bring their sacrifices under their green tree at midnight, then lie to their children that it was Santa who gave them the gifts. They are practicing Christian heathenism with the lying doctrines of the Devil to deceive children. I have used the term "Lying Christian Heathen" not because one can simultaneously be a Christian and a heathen. But, because of the shift in Christianity in this End-Time, where everyone claims to be a Christian. In 2016, if I remember the year correctly, I saw a flyer for the "Christian Witches Conference" to be held somewhere in Salem, Massachusetts. If witches claim to be Christians, the heathens, likewise, do the same. They all call themselves Christians and practice the Christmas heathenism; they are lying Christian heathens. That is what backslidden Christians do; they nominally claim Christianity while dining at the tables of devils.

Jeremiah 3:6

The Lord said also unto me in the days of Josiah the king, Hast thou seen that which backsliding Israel hath done? she is gone up upon every high mountain and under every green tree, and there hath played the harlot.

Jeremiah 10:1-4

[1]Hear ye the word which the LORD speaketh unto you, O house of Israel: [2]Thus saith the LORD, Learn not the way of the heathen, and be not dismayed at the signs of heaven; for the heathen are dismayed at them. [3]For the customs of the people are vain: for one cutteth a tree out of the forest, the work of the hands of the workman, with the axe. [4]They deck it with silver and with gold; they fasten it with nails and with hammers, that it move not.

The Empirical Evidence

The Bible says that those who are amazed by the signs of heaven, cut trees and deck them with silver and gold, are heathens. God said that the customs of the heathens are vain, meaning they are useless. The same you do, you cut a tree out of the forest, or you buy an already cut one, the handiwork of the workman with an axe. Or you buy a synthetic replica, a plastic one, the handiwork of men. God said, the heathens are fascinated by the signs of heaven, and they deck their fastened cut trees with silver and gold. Is that not what you do with your green trees? You beautify it with silver and golden images, representing all kinds of heavenly signs; the sun, the moon, and lights for the stars. You deck it to be very colorful and appealing to the eyes. Then, at midnight, before the dawn of December 25th, when no one is watching. You secretly drop sacrifices, "gifts" under your green tree for your idol, Santa Claus, Satan. Who will be glorified on the morning of Christmas as the giver of the gifts, the rewarder. That is what backslidden children of God do. Jeremiah 3:6, *"The Lord said also unto me in the days of Josiah the king, Hast thou seen that which backsliding Israel hath done? she is gone up upon every high mountain and under every green tree, and there hath played the harlot.* 2 Chronicles 28:4, *"He sacrificed also and burnt incense in the high places, and on the hills, and under every green tree."* Then, in the morning, you lie to your children that Santa flew from the North Pole, came in through the chimney at midnight, and left them the gifts. The children wake up in the morning to find plenty of sacrifices to enjoy, and feast on in the house of their lord, Santa, Satan. Just like when the children of Israel go for their sacrifices to the LORD, and there is plenty to feast on. Your children wake up and see that there are plenty of sacrifices that have been made under this green tree for them to enjoy and be merry.

You lie to the children continually that their god, Santa Claus, flew from the North Pole at night, where he exalted himself. Then flew through the air like the prince of the power of the air, Satan, "the spirit that works in the children of disobedience." Passed through your chimney at midnight when they were sleeping and dropped these gifts, "sacrifices" for them to enjoy on the morning of December 25th. Your children rejoice, and give thanks and glory to Santa Claus, Old Nick the Devil. They jubilate, celebrate, and testify to the goodness of Santa to everyone who would care to listen to know what Santa gave them for Christmas. Santa gave me this, and Santa gave me that for Christmas! All to the glory of Santa Claus, Satan, the god of Christmas. But God had said, *"I am the LORD: that is my name: and my glory will I not give to another, neither my praise to graven images."* Isaiah 42:8. But you have sacrificed to your god, Satan, and preached his lying doctrine to your children to glorify him in place of God. You have given God's glory and praise to another god and deceitfully caused your children to do the same. You are a lying Christian heathen.

2 Kings 16:3-4

³But he walked in the way of the kings of Israel, yea, and made his son to pass through the fire, according to the abominations of the heathen, whom the LORD cast out from before the children of Israel. ⁴And he sacrificed and burnt incense in the high places, and on the hills, and under every green tree.

Jeremiah 3:6-8

⁶The Lord said also unto me in the days of Josiah the king, Hast thou seen that which backsliding Israel hath done? she is gone up upon every high mountain and under every green tree, and there hath played the harlot. ⁷And I said after she had done all these things, Turn thou unto me. But she returned not. And her treacherous sister Judah saw it. ⁸And I saw, when for all the causes whereby backsliding Israel committed adultery I had put her away, and given her a bill of divorce; yet her treacherous sister Judah feared not, but went and played the harlot also.

This is what backsliding children of God do. This is what the backslidden kings in Israel did; this is the character of backslidden people who have forgotten God, who have turned away from God. They fall back to heathenism and practice the green tree heathenistic sacrifice rituals. Satan has tricked you into doing the same in the name of celebrating the birthday of Jesus Christ, which was not meant to be celebrated. You have fallen back to heathenism and are practicing the same heathenistic green tree rituals. Do you still think that you are a Christian, while your heathenistic works belie the faith you proclaim? Would you still call yourself a Christian? Yes, nominally, you are a Christian. However, nominal Christianity is for backslidden children of God; it will not save you at the end. Satan and his minister are also normal Christians. They also believe in Jesus; they believe that He is the Son of God, and they tremble.

James 2:18-19

[18]Yea, a man may say, Thou hast faith, and I have works: shew me thy faith without thy works, and I will shew thee my faith by my works. [19]Thou believest that there is one God; thou doest well: the devils also believe, and tremble.

Matthew 8:28-29

[28]And when he was come to the other side into the country of the Gergesenes, there met him two possessed with devils, coming out of the tombs, exceeding fierce, so that no man might pass by that way. [29]And, behold, they cried out, saying, What have we to do with thee, Jesus, thou Son of God? art thou come hither to torment us before the time?

2 Corinthians 11:13-15

[11]For such are false apostles, deceitful workers, transforming themselves into the apostles of Christ. [14]And no marvel; for Satan himself is transformed into an angel of light. [15]Therefore it is no great thing if his ministers also be transformed as the ministers of righteousness; whose end shall be according to their works.

Satan and his ministers are Christians in name only – nominal Christians. They won't be saved, because they are not practicing Christians. Though they transform themselves into angels and ministers of light, deceitfully preaching and teaching the Word of God. They will not be saved because they don't obey the Word of God. The backslidden Christians are nominal Christians, just like the backslidden Israelites are Jews in name only. Nominal Christians are not Word Practitioners; they don't practice the Word of God as it is in the Bible. They sacrifice under every green tree on December 25th, just like the heathens do. They sacrifice under their green Christmas tree at home, in their churches, and everywhere. They make sacrifices at midnight under their green trees to Santa, i.e., Satan, in the form of Christmas gifts. Then, in the morning, they lie to their children and give the glory to their god, Satan, Lucifer, Old Nick the Devil, called Santa Claus, or Father Christmas. They are lying Christian heathens, and their heathenistic works belie the Christian faith they proclaim. They surely will not be saved at the end, except they repent.

Exodus 32:8-10

[8]They have turned aside quickly out of the way which I commanded them: they have made them a molten calf, and have worshipped it, and have sacrificed thereunto, and said, These be thy gods, O Israel, which have brought thee up out of the land of Egypt. [9]And the LORD said unto Moses, I have seen this people, and, behold, it is a stiffnecked people: [10]Now therefore let me alone, that my wrath may wax hot against them, and that I may consume them: and I will make of thee a great nation.

The lying Christian heathens have quickly turned away from the way of the LORD, just like the backslidden children of Israel at Mount Sinai. Applying their heathenistic practices to amplify Exodus 32:8 clearly shows that they are practicing the same idolatry as the Israelites did at Mount Sinai. Exodus 32:8, *"They have turned aside quickly out of the way which I commanded them* (they have turned away from the way of God's Word (Bible) which did not teach them to celebrate Christmas; and condemned the heathenistic green tree sacrifice)*: they have made them a molten calf* (they have created the fictitious Santa Claus, the false god)*, and have worshipped it* (they have made wishes and prayers to Santa for Christmas gifts and given thanks and praises to him for the gifts), *and have sacrificed thereunto* (they have dropped Christmas gifts under their Christmas green tree at midnight in the name of Santa), *and said, These be thy gods, O Israel, which have brought thee up out of the land of Egypt* (they said to their children this is thy gift from your god, Santa Claus, who have rewarded you for being good). *"*

9.3: The Consequences Of Believing In Fictitious Santa

Santa Claus is a fictitious being with attributes similar to those of God. He is an imaginary being made to rob God of his glory and to sit above the congregation of Jesus Christ, the church, just like Satan desires. Children will forever remember all the lies their lying Christian heathen parents had told them about the fictitious Santa. And this most often results in damnable consequences in their adulthood. These parents' sinful practices of lying and their heathenistic green tree sacrifice rituals will be engraved with a diamond pen on their children's hearts. The children most likely will not deviate from it, and it will ultimately lead to their spiritual/eternal death. It will eventually lead them to heathenism, atheism, and to hating God. Just like the children of the backslidden Jewish heathens remember their altars, and their groves by the green trees upon the high hills. They did not forget because it was engraved on their hearts with a diamond pen. Likewise, the children of the lying Christian heathens will remember the green tree altars and sacrifices, and all the lies they were told about the fictitious Santa. It will be engraved on their hearts with a diamond pen.

The Empirical Evidence

Jeremiah 17:1-2

¹The sin of Judah is written with a pen of iron, and with the point of a diamond: it is graven upon the table of their heart, and upon the horns of your altars; ²Whilst their children remember their altars and their groves by the green trees upon the high hills.

Lying Christian heathen parents continuously lie to their innocent children about the fictitious Satan. They lie to their children that if they are good, Santa Claus will give them gifts for Christmas. On Christmas morning, they lie that at midnight Santa Claus flew down from the North Pole through the chimney to leave gifts for them under the green tree. The innocent children wholeheartedly believe all the lies they were told about Santa, not knowing that Santa Claus is a fictitious figure. Remember that they have been teaching their children about Jesus Christ, whose birthday the children associate with Santa Claus. The children are deceived; they believe with their whole heart that Santa is real. They earnestly make wishes and prayers to Santa Claus with all their heart for the gifts they desire. Santa Claus answers their prayer and gives them their heart's desires. The children rejoice and give thanks to Santa for answering their prayers and rewarding them for being good. They love Santa and believe in him with all their hearts because their trusted parents told them he is real. Then, only to find out many years later, as they grow up, that Santa is not real. Oh! "My trusted parents have deceived me all these years." Santa is a fictitious character. Oh, they told me that Santa only comes to reward those who are good. They use it to deceive me into behaving. And because Santa Claus, whom their trusted parents had deceived them about, is associated with Jesus and Christianity. Therefore, the children will draw these conclusions. Hmm! If Santa, who brings gifts to me on Jesus' birthday, is a fictitious character, then Jesus must also be a fictitious character. If Santa, a fictitious character, is used to talk about a Jesus that I have never seen, then Jesus is surely a fictitious character. I see! The Bible stories are not real; Christianity is just a religion of lies used to make children behave and be good. The story about God, the Bible, is all a myth, an old folk's tale, Jesus is not real, just like Santa. That is the argument and conclusions that the hearts of the children would adopt by default as a result of this deception.

Have you seen one of the reasons why children of this generation do not regard the Bible as the Word of God? Do you now understand why there are so many arguments against the inerrancy of the Word of God, even by those raised in the church? They argue that the Bible is not the Word of God; it is a book written by men. You must have heard such arguments. These lying Christian heathen parents have contributed much to this outcome. They have lied to their children for many years about a fictitious Santa. The children's conclusion is simple yet resolute. If my trusted parents could tell me these lies about Santa with all seriousness for so long. Now, are they telling me more tales about fictitious characters in the Bible, about God, to make me morally good? These old folks just want people to behave and live an obedient and morally upright life. They will reject the Bible as the inerrant Word of God and treat Christianity as every other mythology. All things being equal, those children will become atheists or, at best, lying Christian heathens like their parents, to their spiritual and eternal death.

Part 3

THE

REVELATIONAL

EVIDENCE

CHAPTER 10

GOD'S REVELATIONS ON CHRISTMAS CELEBRATION

I n this part, we will affirm the truth about the December 25th Christmas celebration through revelations. Genuine revelations are God's Word to His people in the present. They could either come through prophecies, dreams, visions, or an audible voice. Genuine revelations will not contradict God's Word; they always validate and give clarity to God's written words in the Bible. Any revelation that contradicts the Bible is not from God. The Bible is our USA, i.e., "Ultimate Source of Authority," for reference to truth. The truth about Christianity and life in general is found in the Bible. The Bible is a compilation of God's revelations to forty different authors of various backgrounds and geographic locations over a period of about 1,500 years. The Bible, "Basic Instruction Before Leaving Earth," is God's Word to humanity. It is the book that reveals all the truth about life and its purpose. All truth claims in life that contradict the Bible are false claims, be they religious or scientific. The Bible validates the authenticity and relevance of revelations and prophecies in contemporary times.

John 16:13-14

13Howbeit when he, the Spirit of truth, is come, he will guide you into all truth: for he shall not speak of himself; but whatsoever he shall hear, that shall he speak: and he will shew you things to come. 14He shall glorify me: for he shall receive of mine, and shall shew it unto you.

1 Thessalonians 5:19-21

19Quench not the Spirit. 20Despise not prophesyings. 21Prove all things; hold fast that which is good.

Jesus says in John 16 that He will send us, His followers, the Spirit of truth to guide us into all truth. He said that the Spirit will not speak anything contrary to the course of Jesus Christ, and will only glorify Him. Then, in Thessalonians 5, Christians were admonished not to quench the Spirit of truth and should not despise prophecies. They should prove all prophecies and hold on to good prophecies, i.e., those in line with the Bible. However, some Christians claim that prophecies and revelations ended with the Apostles and have ceased after the Apostolic era. This is a false claim because it contradicts the Bible and the very essence of Jesus Christ, and does not glorify Him. Hebrews 13:8, *"Jesus Christ the same yesterday, and to day, and for ever."* The Bible says that Jesus is the same yesterday, today, and forever. Therefore, if He gave revelations yesteryears during the Apostolic era, He will also give revelations today because He is the same forever. Jesus said that when the Holy Spirit comes, He will speak, John 16:13. *"Howbeit when he, the Spirit of truth, is come, he will guide you into all truth: for he shall not speak of himself; but whatsoever he shall hear, that shall he speak: and he will shew you things to come."* Then, how come these Christians are claiming that the Holy Spirit can no longer speak?

The question should be, what has the Holy Spirit revealed in our time about the December 25th Christmas celebrations? I have enjoyed the privilege of receiving revelations from God myself. Mostly, God gives me revelations through dreams, an audible voice, and prophecies. God has given me many revelations, including those about the Rapture. God has guided me in my spiritual journey through many revelations, validating and clarifying His Word in the Bible to guide me into all truth. Through revelations, God has often rebuked and instructed me in my Christian journey. Therefore, the importance of prophecies and revelations in the Christian journey is astronomical. In this chapter, we will validate the biblical truth of Christmas celebrations with two divine revelations. These divine revelations were given to Mrs. Josephine Ihejirika.

10.1: Divine Revelation On Christmas Celebration

This prophetic revelation on Christmas celebration was given to Mrs. Josephine Ihejirika in 2016. Josephine was born in Imo State, Nigeria, and currently lives in Massachusetts, USA. She was married to the late Mr. Anthony Ihejirika. She is my mother, and we, the children, took our last name, McAnthony, from our father's name, meaning "Son of Anthony." If there is a person that I could stake my life on, in trusting their prophecies and revelations to be directly from God, it would be my mother. She has an extraordinary gift of hearing from God. One that I have never seen or heard of in anyone else in our time. I bear witness to her unhypocritical Christian life, her fear of God, and her commitment to the course of Christ. Before I came to the LORD, God had used her to reveal some of my evil deeds, some even before I actually did them. It was her genuine Christian life and God's extraordinary gifts and presence with her that convinced me that God truly exists and rules over the affairs of men. This led to my total surrender to God and to His guidance in life. God had spoken to me, the family, and the church through her for the umpteenth time about past, present, and future events. To guide, protect, comfort, and save from destruction. Here is the prophetic revelation God gave her in 2016 concerning the December 25th Christmas celebration. She added the Scriptures as references to what the LORD was saying.

At the early hours of the morning, while I was praying, I was about to round up my prayers before the LORD God began to ask me the following questions: If someone has rejected praying with the rosary but still prays through Mary and asks Mary to help them. What is the difference between the person who is praying with the rosary and praying through Mary? I responded and answered that there is no difference. And the LORD asked me another question. He said, 'If someone, whether a pastor or anyone else, tells you that Jesus Christ will come in January, will you believe or agree with them?' I said no, and He asked me why? I answered that the Bible did not tell us the date Jesus Christ will come. He added that if I later decide to prepare for the coming of Jesus Christ based on the date the person or pastor has given earlier. It is the same thing as any believer who is fully aware that there is nowhere in the Bible that gives the date the LORD Jesus Christ was born, and prepares for Christmas by giving gifts and accepting gifts, or any other preparation for Christmas. Luke 2:1-20, Luke1:31-35. Isa 7:14, Isa 9:6-7, Matt 1:18-25, Matt 2:1-end, Deuteronomy 18:18-19, Rev12:5, Micah 5:2.

He also said that any believer who celebrates Christmas is a deceiver and is not telling people the truth. He admonished His children and all believers to stop where the Bible has stopped. He said the purpose Jesus Christ came into the world was to redeem or save the whole world from their sins, and for them to receive Him as their personal LORD and Savior, and not to celebrate His birthday. He also said that, if He, the God Almighty, wanted the world to know the date Jesus Christ was born, He would have told Isaiah the Prophet. Every believer should stop deceiving people by celebrating Christmas or telling them the date. They should tell the truth and the purpose Jesus came by preaching Christ to the whole world. He said that He only commanded His disciples to do the Passover in remembrance of Him. Luke 22:15-22, 1Cor 11:23-26. He added that His people have forsaken the remembrance of His death and resurrection, and they have chosen to celebrate Christmas instead of preaching His salvation and resurrection to the whole world. Matt 17:22-23, Matt 28:1-10, 18-20, Mark 16:1-9,15-19, Luke 9:22, Luke 24:1-9,18-33, John 20:1-21.

The LORD had spoken to her on the December 25th Christmas celebration because she had earlier received Christmas gifts from people in the church. At that time, we were worshipping in the Redeemed Christian Church of God (RCCG). After the LORD had finished speaking to her about Christmas. The LORD asked her to return the Christmas gifts she had received and commanded her never to accept Christmas gifts. And not to receive Christmas wishes and greetings from people, but to tell them that Christmas is not from Him. Therefore, for Heavenly-minded Christians, the matter of Christmas celebration is a serious and consequential one. The prudent ones will hide themselves from the evil of Christmas to protect themselves from God's judgment. But the simple-hearted will say, What does it matter? We are just celebrating the birth of our Savior, Jesus Christ. Proverbs 22:3, *"A prudent man foreseeth the evil, and hideth himself: but the simple pass on, and are punished."*

10.2: The Conclusion Of The Whole Matter

The outline for this book was set up to have a conclusion from the onset. This is the first book that I have set up to have a conclusion. And as I wrote, I kept on reasoning whether it is necessary to have a conclusion. However, when I started writing the revelational evidence. Then I realized, to my greatest surprise, that God had already given me the conclusion. I was really amazed and gave glory to God Almighty, who has been involved in the writing of this book from the very start. God gave me this conclusion on my birthday on August 30, 2025. I guess He must have given me a birthday gift. I had asked my mother earlier that day if the LORD had said anything else to her on Christmas that I might include in this book, apart from the one from 2016, which was written down. She said there is nothing else besides the one from 2016. Then later in the night, around 8 pm, the LORD spoke to her by prophecy and gave her this concluding message to give me. The message never came across to me as the conclusion of this book until I got to this part in October. What other conclusion would I have given that would have been better than the one God gave? The LORD gave a chilling conclusion in the strongest words possible. It caused me to fear God the more and to realign my previous conclusions on the Christmas celebrations with the LORD's message. Here is the message that the LORD gave me on August 30, 2025, on the conclusion of the whole matter about Christmas:

There's no place I commanded My children to celebrate Christmas, from Genesis to Revelation. I never commanded any of My twelve Apostles to celebrate Christmas. Even John the beloved, whom I gave much revelation, I did not add the celebration of Christmas in the revelation. Paul the Apostle, whom I met on the road to Damascus, whom I brought in at last, I did not instruct him to celebrate Christmas. All Bishops, General Overseers, Presidents, and Church Founders, both great and small, who have said that they will celebrate Christmas. They should read the Bible from Genesis to Revelation. When they are done with their celebrations, they will tell Me where in the Bible they saw it that made them celebrate, and recommend it. And if there is no place they saw it, My Word is settled in heaven. It is with My Word that I judge people. These My Words will judge such a person: John 12:47-48; Revelation 22:18-19; Psalm 119:89; Deuteronomy 4:2; Deuteronomy 12:32; Proverbs 30:6; Ecclesiastes 3:14.

John 12:47-48

⁴⁷And if any man hear my words, and believe not, I judge him not: for I came not to judge the world, but to save the world. ⁴⁸He that rejecteth me, and receiveth not my words, hath one that judgeth him: the word that I have spoken, the same shall judge him in the last day.

Revelation 22:18-19

²²For I testify unto every man that heareth the words of the prophecy of this book, If any man shall add unto these things, God shall add unto him the plagues that are written in this book: ¹⁹And if any man shall take away from the words of the book of this prophecy, God shall take away his part out of the book of life, and out of the holy city, and from the things which are written in this book.

Psalm 119:89

For ever, O LORD, thy word is settled in heaven.

Deuteronomy 4:2

Ye shall not add unto the word which I command you, neither shall ye diminish ought from it, that ye may keep the commandments of the LORD your God which I command you.

Deuteronomy 12:32

What thing soever I command you, observe to do it: thou shalt not add thereto, nor diminish from it.

Proverbs 30:6

Add thou not unto his words, lest he reprove thee, and thou be found a liar.

Ecclesiastes 3:14

I know that, whatsoever God doeth, it shall be for ever: nothing can be put to it, nor any thing taken from it: and God doeth it, that men should fear before him.

It's with My Word that I judge people. It is with it that I judged the two sons of Aaron in Leviticus 10:1-3, because they offered strange fire which I have not commanded. That is the nature of My Word. My Word says that the things revealed belong to My children in the world to keep them with their children from generation to generation (Deuteronomy 29:29). That is My Word, which I have revealed to them, as they see in the Bible. But this one, which I hid and did not reveal to Isaiah. And there is no place where I commanded it in the Bible, from Genesis to Revelation. Whoever says that it is the most important one for them to practice, it is Satan deceiving them. Whenever they are done, all these My Words will judge them in the last day. I will judge them the same way I judged Aaron's children, who added to My Word. Therefore, with boldness, tell My children, and people you relate with who celebrate Christmas, that Christmas is not from Me. That I did not command My disciples, and have not commanded this generation to celebrate Christmas. I will not water down My Word. I will not amend My Word for any generation. I will not remove from My Word. And anyone who amends and removes from it; these My Words will judge them in the last day. Thus sayeth the LORD.

They said a word is enough for the wise, and I believe that heaven-minded Christians have heard what the Spirit says. Revelation 3:22, *"He that hath an ear, let him hear what the Spirit saith unto the churches."* The early church never celebrated the birthday of Jesus Christ. It was Satan that brought in the December 25th Christmas celebration into Christendom through the Catholic church. Most true and holy church denominations in contemporary times did not celebrate Christmas in their early years. They resisted and preached against Christmas celebrations. They raised fences by organizing crusades/conferences during the Christmas season to protect their member from the Christmas celebrations. However, today, some of these same holiness churches, as well as newer ones, have turned a blind eye to Christmas celebrations. They have torn down the fences that their fathers had set up to protect the Church. Proverbs 22:28, *"Remove not the ancient landmark, which thy fathers have set."* It is said that before you tear down a fence, pause long enough to find out why it was set up in the first place. May the LORD build His Church and let not the gates of hell prevail against it, in Jesus' name, AMEN.

OTHER BOOKS WRITTEN BY THE AUTHOR

1. TRUMP THE GREAT! THE 45TH & 47TH PRESIDENT OF THE UNITED STATES. GOD'S END-TIME VESSEL

Amazon Reviews On Trump The Great!:

1. Angel59: Second coming of Christ

This book opened my eyes to how close our lord Jesus is coming soon. The current events are just the beginning of what's to come.

2. Lala: Very Insightful, Second Coming Of Jesus Christ!

Just finished this book, great read!

The storytelling, insight, humor, humility, and scriptural relations in the writing are remarkable. The style of writing is engaging, I love the way the book ended, the very last page.

We choose you, President Donald J Trump!

TRUMPITO, we stand with you! Much love from New Jersey! #MAGA #TRUMPFOREVERYONE

WHEN JESUS SAYS YES, NOBODY CAN SAY NO!

THE KINGDOM OF GOD IS AT HAND, REPENT AND WALK WITH THE LORD IN HOLINESS AND RIGHTEOUSNESS TODAY!

3. Kindle Customer: The expectations of the righteous shall not be cut off

This is a striking representation and cover. The title says it all. God is truly at work, and anyone who knows that there is a creator and men are the creatures should venture to read this book. A well-thought-out book that flows with the sequence.

4. OG: Wow!

This indeed is the revelation of God to His children. Never in my years of reading the Bible have I understood the excerpt of scriptures cited in this book; the 7 days of creation and its relation to the time of Christ's coming. I am baffled at the author's understanding of the scripture, and I am convinced that this is the Lord's doing. Indeed, He revealed secret things to them that fear Him. This is a strong wake-up call to me and Christians who await the rapture. It is all a cry unto sinners to come to Christ. I am blessed beyond words! I started this book as I woke up this morning because I had the burden to read it since yesterday, for what reason, I don't know, but now I know. I started reading this book and never dropped it till I finished it, I never wanted it to finish. This is a great evangelism tool. God bless the author, Pastor Cliff McAnthony. More grace! Maranatha!

5. *Roxen Herman: A Must Read!*

Very insightful and scripturally accurate. I highly recommend purchasing this book, you won't be disappointed.

2. THE STORY OF JESUS COLORING BOOK

Amazon Reviews on The Story of Jesus Coloring Book:

1. *Chidu: Buy it and enjoy it*

Children and adults alike would enjoy the simple easy to follow truth of God's word.

3. THE STORY OF DANIEL COLORING BOOK

No available Amazon Reviews for The Story of Daniel Coloring Book:

4. KIDIFFIED

Amazon Reviews on KIDDIFIED:

1. *Sonia: GET THIS BOOK NOW*

This OUTSTANDING book presents a provocative and deeply spiritual perspective on the influence of modern culture on children. It challenges parents to rethink the seemingly harmless terminology we use to refer to our children, such as calling them "kids" — a term that, may unconsciously link them to symbolic associations with goats, sin offerings, and even Satanic practices. Reading this book shows you how, Satan has infiltrated the nurturing environment meant to guide children in godliness, instead turning them into "kiddified" souls disconnected from God.

This book posits that modern media — including social media, music, TV, cartoons, and video games — serves as a vehicle for spiritual harm, conditioning children to be rebellious, selfish, and indifferent to the divine. One of the book's core messages is that parents need to take back control over their children's upbringing, particularly during the most formative years. The author urges parents to be vigilant in guarding their children's hearts and minds against the pernicious influence of secularism, materialism, and Satanic ideologies. The author challenges readers to reconsider the sources of influence in their children's lives and to actively cultivate a spiritual environment where children can grow in their faith and knowledge of God.

Ultimately, this book is a wake-up call for Christian parents, urging them to evaluate how they are raising their children in a world filled with distractions and subtle spiritual dangers. I WILL HIGHLY RECOMMEND THIS TO EVERYONE.

2. Gabriel: A diagnostic, problem-solving masterpiece!

I highly recommend this book. They say, a problem discovered is a problem half-solved.

As a school teacher, I see firsthand the effect of words on children. Words are prophetic. They can build up a life or tear it down.

If every parent, leader, carer, adult, and child (those that can read) in our world reads this book and makes the necessary, recommended changes to their vocabulary and practices, our world will be a way better place!

I highly recommend this book!

5. PRINCIPLES OF RAISING GODLY CHILDREN

Amazon Reviews on Principles of Raising Godly Children:

1. Heine: This book will open your eyes!

I cannot recall how many lightbulb moments I had while going through this inspired book.

Nothing we have, besides children, are of eternal value - nothing! This book shone the light on this. Our Almighty Father has used pastor Cliff to reprove, rebuke, correct, instruct, inspire, and encourage us to do what is right for ourselves, and our children, for the Lord WILL hold us accountable.

There are many things we do not consider strongly when it comes to our children, some through carelessness, while others through ignorance. This book addresses the open doors we have in our lives that satan uses to get at our children.

Matthew 10:16 (KJV)

Behold, I send you forth as sheep in the midst of wolves: be ye therefore wise as serpents, and harmless as doves.

I'm blessed by the wisdom in this book, to overcome the strategies, devices, and snares of Satan; there are many more than

Christmas!

I knew before. We are in the endtimes and must be watchful, for it is getting worse, daily.

I just bought a copy for a friend, and will gift others, as the Lord gives me the grace. I am sure you would do the same after reading this book.

More grace to you, sir, for this book. The Lord will reward you.

2. Gabe: Children are the only durable asset you possess
Wow! Wow!! Wow!!!

Where has this book been?! Why isn't it in every library, school, office, and home?! Wow! The most valuable things are truly hidden in plain sight.

I highly recommend this book for every parent, teacher, pastor, youth pastor, counsellor, coach...literally anyone that has to interact with children. This book is diagnostic and therapeutic in every sense of it. If you understand the root cause of a problem, then you'd be sure to solve it.

"Early years psychology says, give me a child from ages 0-7 and I'll make him whatever you want him to be!" For a long time, parents haven't paid much attention to training their children during these most crucial early years. It's hard and nearly impossible to build a desired, dependable, durable house on a faulty foundation.

It's time to start building (training) early from ground zero, folks. Get this book now and get some for your friends and loved ones who are experiencing the same struggles with raising godly children in today's world!

Gabriel
School Teacher,
Queensland, Australia